Contents

• • • • • • • • •

Page 57

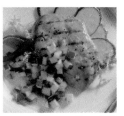

Page 141

Page 217

Page 317

Page 101

Page 181

Page 343

3

Introduction

Light cooking is more than just a passing fad—it's the new way of life in today's health-conscious society. Quick weight loss schemes may be tempting, but they often produce little more than short-lived and ultimately disappointing results. The alternative choice—learning healthy cooking and eating habits—is an important lifestyle change with long-lasting and far-reaching benefits. Fortunately, developing these habits does *not* mean eating very small quantities of food with very little flavor. This spectacular collection of recipes contains everything from savory, party-perfect appetizers to rich chocolate desserts, most with under 300 calories and 10 grams of fat or less per serving!

Calories, fat and cholesterol are major factors in healthy eating, of course, but it is important to look at them as part of the bigger picture and not just as independent values that need changing. The U.S. Department of Agriculture and the Department of Health and Human Services have developed a Food Guide Pyramid to illustrate how easy it is to eat a healthier diet. It is not a rigid prescription, but rather a general guide that lets you choose a healthful diet that's right for you. It calls for eating a wide variety of foods to get the nutrients you need, and, at the same time, the right amount of calories to maintain a healthy weight.

Food Guide Pyramid
A Guide to Daily Food Choices

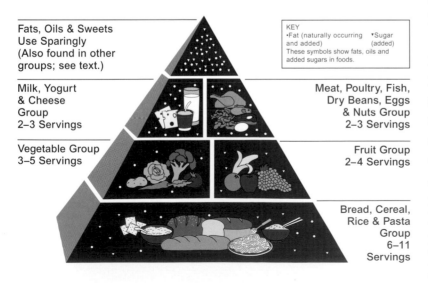

Fats, Oils & Sweets
Use Sparingly
(Also found in other groups; see text.)

KEY
•Fat (naturally occurring and added)   ▼Sugar (added)
These symbols show fats, oils and added sugars in foods.

Milk, Yogurt & Cheese Group
2–3 Servings

Meat, Poultry, Fish, Dry Beans, Eggs & Nuts Group
2–3 Servings

Vegetable Group
3–5 Servings

Fruit Group
2–4 Servings

Bread, Cereal, Rice & Pasta Group
6–11 Servings

The amount of fat in our diets has become a primary concern, and with very good reason. High-fat diets have been linked with increased blood cholesterol levels (which in turn produce greater risk for heart disease) as well as increased risks for obesity and some types of cancers. Nutrition experts recommend diets that contain 30% or less of total daily calories from fat, a goal that applies to a total diet over time rather than a single food or meal. Reaching this goal simply requires making smart choices—and having the information to make these choices.

FAVORITE BRAND NAME

BEST-LOVED

LIGHT

• RECIPES •

PUBLICATIONS INTERNATIONAL, LTD.

Front cover photography: Peter Walters Photography, Chicago

Pictured on the front cover *(clockwise from right):* Grilled Chicken Sienna *(page 162)*, Athenian Rice with Feta Cheese *(page 276)* and Luscious Chocolate Cheesecake *(page 312)*.

Pictured on the back cover *(clockwise from top right):* Black Forest Chocolate Fudge Cake *(page 288)*, Fresh Vegetable Lasagna *(page 282)*, Nacho Salad *(page 230)* and Margarita Pork Kabobs *(page 104)*.

ISBN: 0-7853-2645-6

Library of Congress Catalog Card Number: 96-69846

Manufactured in U.S.A.

8 7 6 5 4 3 2 1

Nutritional Analysis: In the case of multiple choices, the first ingredient, the lowest amount and the lowest serving yield are used to calculate the nutritional analysis. "Serve with" suggestions are not included unless otherwise stated.

Microwave Cooking: Microwave ovens vary in wattage. The microwave cooking times given in this publication are approximate. Use the cooking times as guidelines and check for doneness before adding more time. Consult manufacturer's instructions for suitable microwave-safe cooking dishes.

The Healthy Choice® recipes contained in this book have been tested by the manufacturers and have been carefully edited by the publisher. The publisher and the manufacturer cannot be held responsible for any ill effects caused by errors in the recipes, or by spoiled ingredients, unsanitary conditions, incorrect preparation procedures or any other cause.

Many lower fat options are already popular choices at the supermarket, such as nonfat or low-fat dairy products, lean meats and skinless chicken. Other healthy choices include a wide range of complex carbohydrates, such as grains, beans, fruits and vegetables. These may be eaten in larger quantities than high-fat foods because a gram of fat contains nine calories while a gram of carbohydrate or protein contains only four. Thus a large, filling, low-fat salad or baked potato might have the same number of calories as a tiny portion of potato chips, which is usually consumed quickly and leaves people hungry for more.

The recipes in this book are designed to help you with these choices, while proving that the good-for-you dishes can be the good tasting ones as well. Choose from hundreds of flavorful low-calorie, low-fat recipes—from appetizers to desserts, from breakfast to dinner and everything in between. The nutritional information that follows each recipe tells you the number of calories, the grams (g) of fat, the milligrams (mg) of cholesterol and the milligrams (mg) of sodium per serving. Most recipes contain less than 300 calories and 10 grams of fat or less per serving, so preparing meals that all fit into a healthy lifestyle has never been easier!

About the Nutritional Information

The analysis of each recipe includes all the ingredients that are listed in that recipe, except ingredients labeled as "optional" or "for garnish." If a range is offered for an ingredient (¼ to ½ teaspoon, for example), the *first* amount given was used to calculate the nutritional information. If an ingredient is presented with an option ("2 tablespoons margarine or butter"), the *first* item listed was used to calculate the nutritional information. Foods shown in photographs on the same serving plate and offered as "serve with" suggestions at the end of a recipe are *not* included in the recipe analysis unless it is stated in the per serving line.

The nutritional information that appears with each recipe was submitted in part by the participating companies and associations. Every effort has been made to check the accuracy of these numbers. However, because numerous variables account for a wide range of values for certain foods, nutritive analyses in this book should be considered approximate.

This cookbook offers you a wide variety of recipes that are, on a per serving basis, low in calories, fat and cholesterol. The recipes in this book are NOT intended as a medically therapeutic program, nor as a substitute for medically approved diet plans for people on fat-, cholesterol- or sodium-restricted diets. You should consult your physician before beginning any diet plan. The recipes offered here can be part of a healthy lifestyle that meets recognized dietary guidelines. A healthy lifestyle includes not only eating a balanced diet, but engaging in proper exercise as well.

Appetizers & Beverages

· · · · · · · · · · · ·

Peppy Snack Mix

3	plain rice cakes, broken into bite-size pieces
1½	cups bite-size frosted shredded wheat biscuit cereal
¾	cup pretzel sticks, halved
3	tablespoons reduced-calorie margarine, melted
2	teaspoons low sodium Worcestershire sauce
¾	teaspoon chili powder
⅛	to ¼ teaspoon ground red pepper

Preheat oven to 300°F. Combine rice cakes, wheat biscuits and pretzels in 13×9-inch baking pan. Combine margarine, Worcestershire sauce, chili powder and pepper in small bowl. Drizzle over cereal mixture; toss to coat. Bake, uncovered, 20 minutes, stirring after 10 minutes.   *Makes 6 servings (4 cups)*

NUTRIENTS PER SERVING			
Calories	118	Fat	3 g
Cholesterol	0 mg	Sodium	156 mg

Peppy Snack Mix

Chicken Sesame with Oriental Crème

⅓ cup reduced sodium soy sauce
2 teaspoons minced garlic
1 teaspoon dark sesame oil
½ teaspoon ground ginger
1 pound boneless, skinless chicken breasts, cut into 4×½-inch
    strips
6 ounces (1 carton) ALPINE LACE® Fat Free Cream Cheese
    with Garlic & Herbs
2 tablespoons finely chopped green onions
2 tablespoons sesame seeds, toasted
1 tablespoon extra virgin olive oil

1. To marinate the chicken: In a small bowl, whisk the soy sauce, garlic, sesame oil and ginger. Reserve 2 tablespoons and pour the remaining marinade into a self-sealing plastic bag. Add the chicken pieces and seal the bag. Turn the bag to coat the chicken. Refrigerate for at least 2 hours, turning occasionally.

2. To make the Oriental Crème: In another small bowl, place the cream cheese. Whisk in the reserved 2 tablespoons of marinade and stir in the green onions. Cover with plastic wrap and refrigerate.

3. To prepare the chicken: Remove the chicken from the marinade and discard any remaining marinade. Spread the sesame seeds on a plate and roll the chicken strips in them until lightly coated.

4. In a large nonstick skillet, heat the olive oil over medium-high heat. Add the chicken and stir-fry for 6 minutes or until golden brown and the juices run clear when the chicken is pierced with a fork. Serve with the Oriental Crème.

Makes 24 appetizer servings

NUTRIENTS PER SERVING			
Calories	43	Fat	1 g
Cholesterol	13 mg	Sodium	192 mg

Chicken Sesame with Oriental Crème

Easy Bean Nachos

24 (about 1 ounce) GUILTLESS GOURMET® Baked Tortilla
     Chips (yellow, white or blue corn)
½ cup GUILTLESS GOURMET® Bean Dip (Black or Pinto, mild
     or hot)
¼ cup chopped green onions
¼ cup GUILTLESS GOURMET® Nacho Dip (mild or spicy)
     Chopped red bell pepper strips (optional)

Microwave Directions: Spread tortilla chips on flat microwave-safe plate. Dab 1 teaspoon bean dip on each chip; sprinkle with onions. Dot ½ teaspoon nacho dip on each chip. Microwave on HIGH (100% power) 30 seconds or until nacho dip starts to melt. Serve hot. Garnish with red pepper, if desired.

Makes 24 nachos

Hint: To keep chips crisp and prevent them from getting soggy, microwave each chip separately.

Conventional Directions: Preheat oven to 325°F. Spread tortilla chips on baking sheet. Prepare nachos as directed. Bake about 5 minutes or until nacho dip starts to melt. Serve hot.

NUTRIENTS PER SERVING			
(1 nacho)			
Calories	13	Fat	<1 g
Cholesterol	0 mg	Sodium	40 mg

Top to bottom: Easy Bean Nachos and Chicken Nachos (page 12)

Chicken Nachos

22 (about 1 ounce) GUILTLESS GOURMET® Baked Tortilla
  Chips (yellow, white or blue corn)
½ cup (4 ounces) cooked and shredded boneless chicken breast
¼ cup chopped green onions
¼ cup GUILTLESS GOURMET® Nacho Dip (mild or spicy)
  Sliced green and red chilies (optional)

Microwave Directions: Spread tortilla chips on flat microwave-safe plate. Sprinkle chicken and onions over chips. Place nacho dip in small microwave-safe bowl. Microwave on HIGH (100% power) 30 seconds; pour over chips, chicken and onions. Microwave on HIGH 30 seconds more or until nacho dip starts to bubble. Serve hot. Garnish with chilies, if desired.

Makes 22 nachos

Conventional Directions: Preheat oven to 325°F. Spread tortilla chips on baking sheet. Sprinkle chicken and onions over chips. Heat nacho dip in small saucepan over medium heat until warm; pour over chips, chicken and onions. Bake about 5 minutes or until nacho dip starts to bubble. Serve hot.

NUTRIENTS PER SERVING			
(1 nacho)			
Calories	13	Fat	<1 g
Cholesterol	3 mg	Sodium	24 mg

Pot Stickers

1 boneless, skinless chicken breast, finely chopped
1 cup cooked rice
½ cup finely chopped fresh mushrooms
1 carrot, finely shredded
2 green onions, finely chopped
1 tablespoon white wine
1 teaspoon cornstarch
1 teaspoon dark sesame oil
¼ teaspoon salt
¼ teaspoon ground white pepper
50 wonton skins
5 tablespoons vegetable oil, divided
2½ cups water, divided
Soy sauce, Chinese hot mustard or sweet and sour sauce

Combine chicken, rice, mushrooms, carrot, onions, wine, cornstarch, sesame oil, salt and pepper in medium bowl. Cut corners from wonton skins with knife or round cookie cutter to make circles. Place 1 teaspoon chicken mixture on center of each circle. Fold circles in half, pressing edges together with fork. Heat 1 tablespoon vegetable oil in large skillet until very hot. Place 10 pot stickers in single layer in skillet; fry 2 minutes or until bottoms are golden brown. Add ½ cup water to skillet. Cover and cook 6 to 7 minutes or until water is absorbed. Repeat with remaining pot stickers, adding 1 tablespoon vegetable oil and ½ cup water per batch. Serve warm with your choice of sauce for dipping.

Makes 50 appetizers

NUTRIENTS PER SERVING			
Calories	49	Fat	2 g
Cholesterol	4 mg	Sodium	86 mg

Favorite recipe from **USA Rice Council**

13

Party Chicken Tarts

    2   tablespoons butter or margarine
    1   cup chopped fresh mushrooms
    ¼   cup finely chopped celery
    ¼   cup finely chopped onion
    2   tablespoons all-purpose flour
 1½   cups chopped cooked chicken
    6   tablespoons sour cream
    ½   teaspoon garlic salt
    1   package (10 ounces) flaky refrigerator biscuits
          (10 to 12 count)
        Vegetable cooking spray
    1   tablespoon butter or margarine, melted
        Grated Parmesan cheese

Melt 2 tablespoons butter in large skillet. Add mushrooms, celery and onion; cook and stir 4 to 5 minutes. Sprinkle with flour; stir in chicken and sour cream. Cook until thoroughly heated. Stir in garlic salt; set aside. Cut each biscuit into quarters; press each piece into miniature muffin tins coated with cooking spray to form tart shell. Brush each piece with melted butter. Bake at 400°F 6 minutes. Remove from oven; *reduce oven temperature to 350°F.* Fill each tart with 1 teaspoon chicken mixture; sprinkle with cheese. Bake 14 to 15 minutes more. Serve immediately.   *Makes 40 to 48 appetizers*

Note: For ease in serving at party time, prepare filling ahead and cook tarts 5 minutes. Fill and bake just before serving for best flavor.

NUTRIENTS PER SERVING			
Calories	49	Fat	3 g
Cholesterol	8 mg	Sodium	131 mg

Favorite recipe from **National Broiler Council**

Party Chicken Tarts

Cheesy Potato Skins with Black Beans & Salsa

6   medium potatoes (6 ounces each), baked
¾   cup GUILTLESS GOURMET® Black Bean Dip (mild or spicy)
¾   cup GUILTLESS GOURMET® Nacho Dip (mild or spicy)
¾   cup GUILTLESS GOURMET® Salsa (mild, medium or hot)
¾   cup low fat sour cream
    Fresh cilantro sprigs (optional)

Preheat oven to 400°F. Cut baked potatoes in half lengthwise and scoop out potato pulp, leaving ¼-inch pulp attached to skin (avoid breaking skin). (Save potato pulp for another use, such as mashed potatoes.) Place potato skins on large baking sheet, skin sides down; bake 5 minutes.

Fill each potato skin with 1 tablespoon bean dip and 1 tablespoon nacho dip. Return to oven; bake 10 minutes. Remove from oven; let cool 5 minutes. Dollop 1 tablespoon salsa and 1 tablespoon sour cream onto each potato. Garnish with cilantro, if desired. Serve hot.   *Makes 12 servings*

NUTRIENTS PER SERVING			
(1 potato skin)			
Calories	133	Fat	1 g
Cholesterol	5 mg	Sodium	216 mg

Cheesy Potato Skins with Black Beans & Salsa

16

Ground Turkey Chinese Spring Rolls

1   pound Ground Turkey
1   large clove garlic, minced
1½ teaspoons fresh ginger, minced
2   cups bok choy, sliced paper thin
½   cup thinly sliced green onions
2   tablespoons reduced-sodium soy sauce
1   teaspoon dry sherry or rice wine
1   teaspoon sesame oil
8   sheets phyllo pastry
    Nonstick cooking spray

Preheat oven to 400°F. In medium nonstick skillet, over medium-high heat, cook and stir turkey, garlic and ginger 4 to 5 minutes or until turkey is no longer pink. Drain thoroughly.

In medium-size bowl combine turkey mixture, bok choy, onions, soy sauce, sherry and oil.

On clean, dry counter, layer phyllo sheets into a stack and cut into 2 (18×7-inch) rectangles. Work with one rectangle of phyllo at a time. (Keep remaining phyllo covered with a damp cloth following package instructions.)

Coat half sheet of phyllo with nonstick cooking spray. On counter arrange phyllo sheet so 7-inch side is parallel to counter edge. Place ¼ cup of turkey mixture in 5-inch strip, 1-inch away from bottom and side edges of phyllo. Fold 1-inch bottom edge of phyllo over filling and fold longer edges of phyllo toward center; roll-up, jelly-roll style. Phyllo may break during rolling, but will hold filling once roll is completed.

Repeat process with remaining rectangles of phyllo and filling to make remaining spring rolls. Place rolls, seam-side-down, on 2 (15×10-inch) cookie

continued on page 20

Ground Turkey Chinese Spring Rolls

Ground Turkey Chinese Spring Rolls, continued

sheets coated with nonstick cooking spray. Coat tops of rolls with nonstick cooking spray. Bake 14 to 16 minutes or until rolls are golden brown.

Serve immediately with Chinese mustard, hoisin sauce and additional soy sauce, if desired.   *Makes 16 servings*

NUTRIENTS PER SERVING			
Calories	86	Fat	3 g
Cholesterol	14 mg	Sodium	140 mg

Favorite recipe from **National Turkey Federation**

Herbed Stuffed Tomatoes

15 cherry tomatoes
½ cup 1% low-fat cottage cheese
1 tablespoon thinly sliced green onion
1 teaspoon chopped fresh chervil *or* ¼ teaspoon dried chervil leaves
½ teaspoon chopped fresh dill *or* ⅛ teaspoon dried dill weed
⅛ teaspoon lemon pepper

Cut thin slice off bottom of each tomato. Scoop out pulp with small spoon; discard pulp. Invert tomatoes on paper towels to drain. Combine cottage cheese, green onion, chervil, dill and lemon pepper in small bowl. Spoon into tomatoes. Serve at once or cover and refrigerate up to 8 hours.

Makes 5 servings

NUTRIENTS PER SERVING			
(3 stuffed tomatoes)			
Calories	27	Fat	<1 g
Cholesterol	1 mg	Sodium	96 mg

Herbed Stuffed Tomatoes

Savory Corn Cakes

2 cups all-purpose flour
1 teaspoon baking powder
½ teaspoon salt
2 cups frozen whole kernel corn, thawed
1 cup skim milk
1 cup (4 ounces) shredded smoked Cheddar cheese
2 egg whites, beaten
1 whole egg, beaten
4 green onions, finely chopped
2 cloves garlic, minced
1 tablespoon chili powder
Prepared salsa (optional)

1. Combine flour, baking powder and salt in large bowl with wire whisk. Stir in corn, milk, cheese, egg whites, egg, green onions, garlic and chili powder until well blended.

2. Spray large nonstick skillet with nonstick cooking spray; heat over medium-high heat.

3. Drop batter by ¼ cupfuls into skillet. Cook 3 minutes per side or until golden brown. Serve with prepared salsa.   *Makes 12 cakes*

NUTRIENTS PER SERVING			
(1 cake)			
Calories	152	Fat	3 g
Cholesterol	25 mg	Sodium	227 mg

Savory Corn Cakes

Fiesta Quesadillas with Fruit Salsa

1   can (11 ounces) DOLE® Mandarin Oranges, drained and
      finely chopped
1   tablespoon chopped fresh cilantro or fresh parsley
1   tablespoon lime juice
4   (8-inch) whole wheat or flour tortillas
¾   cup shredded low fat Monterey Jack, mozzarella or Cheddar
      cheese
⅔   cup finely chopped DOLE® Pitted Dates or Chopped Dates or
      finely chopped Pitted Prunes
⅓   cup crumbled feta cheese
2   tablespoons chopped DOLE® Green Onion

• **Combine** mandarin oranges, cilantro and lime juice in small bowl for salsa;
set aside.

• **Place** two tortillas on large baking sheet. Sprinkle half of shredded cheese,
dates, feta and green onion over each tortilla to within ½ inch of edge.

• **Brush** outer ½-inch edge of each tortilla with water. Top with remaining
tortillas; press down edges gently to seal.

• **Bake** at 375°F 5 to 8 minutes or until hot. Cut each quesadilla into 6 wedges.

• **Drain** salsa just before serving, if desired; serve over warm quesadillas.

Makes 6 servings

Prep time: 15 minutes
Bake time: 8 minutes

NUTRIENTS PER SERVING			
Calories	225	Fat	8 g
Cholesterol	22 mg	Sodium	317 mg

Top to bottom: Fresh Garden Dip (page 26)
and Fiesta Quesadillas with Fruit Salsa

24

Fresh Garden Dip

1½ cups fat free or reduced fat mayonnaise
1½ cups shredded DOLE® Carrots
1 cup finely chopped DOLE® Broccoli Florets
⅓ cup finely chopped DOLE® Green Onions
2 teaspoons dried dill weed
¼ teaspoon garlic powder
    DOLE® Broccoli Florets, Cauliflower Florets or Peeled Mini
    Carrots

• **Stir** together mayonnaise, shredded carrots, chopped broccoli, green onions, dill and garlic powder in medium bowl until blended.

• **Spoon** into serving bowl. Cover and chill 1 hour or overnight. Serve with assorted fresh vegetables. Refrigerate any leftovers in airtight container.

Makes 3½ cups

Prep time: 15 minutes
Chill time: 1 hour

NUTRIENTS PER SERVING			
(1 tablespoon)			
Calories	8	Fat	0 g
Cholesterol	0 mg	Sodium	97 mg

Chili con Queso con Surimi

1 cup chopped onion
2 tablespoons olive or vegetable oil
1 can (16 ounces) tomatoes, coarsely chopped
1 can (4 ounces) diced green chilies
8 ounces (2 cups) shredded low-fat or regular Monterey Jack cheese
8 ounces (2 cups) shredded low-fat Cheddar cheese
1 tablespoon cornstarch
8 ounces surimi seafood, flake-style or chunk-style, coarsely chopped

Cook onion in oil in large saucepan over medium heat until tender but not brown, stirring occasionally. Add tomatoes and chilies; bring to a simmer and cook 5 minutes. Meanwhile, toss cheeses with cornstarch; gradually add to tomato mixture and stir until melted. Stir in surimi seafood. Transfer to top of chafing dish or fondue pot (over hot water, alcohol or candle burner) to keep warm. Serve with corn chips, crackers and raw vegetables for dipping.

Makes 4½ cups

NUTRIENTS PER SERVING			
	(1 tablespoon)		
Calories	27	Fat	1 g
Cholesterol	3 mg	Sodium	91 mg

Favorite recipe from **National Fisheries Institute**

Fresh Tomato Eggplant Spread

1   medium eggplant
2   large ripe tomatoes, seeded and chopped
1   cup minced zucchini
¼   cup chopped green onions with tops
2   tablespoons red wine vinegar
1   tablespoon olive oil
1   teaspoon honey
1   clove garlic, minced
1   tablespoon minced fresh basil
2   teaspoons minced fresh oregano
1   teaspoon minced fresh thyme
⅛   teaspoon ground black pepper
¼   cup pine nuts or slivered almonds
32 melba toast rounds

1. Preheat oven to 375°F. Poke holes in surface of eggplant with fork. Bake 20 to 25 minutes or until tender. Cool completely; peel and mince. Place in colander; press to release excess water.

2. Combine eggplant with tomatoes, zucchini, green onions, vinegar, oil, honey, garlic, basil, oregano, thyme and black pepper in large bowl. Mix well. Refrigerate 2 hours to allow flavors to blend.

3. Stir in pine nuts just before serving. Serve with melba toast rounds.

Makes 8 servings

NUTRIENTS PER SERVING			
Calories	117	Fat	4 g
Cholesterol	0 mg	Sodium	65 mg

Fresh Tomato Eggplant Spread

Festive Chicken Dip

1½ pounds boneless, skinless chicken breasts, finely chopped
    (about 3 cups)
¼ cup lime juice, divided
2 garlic cloves, minced
1 teaspoon salt
½ teaspoon ground black pepper
1 can (16 ounces) refried beans
1½ cups sour cream, divided
1 package (1¼ ounces) dry taco seasoning mix, divided
1 tablespoon picante sauce
1 avocado, chopped
1 tablespoon olive oil
1 cup (4 ounces) shredded sharp Cheddar cheese
1 small onion, finely chopped
2 tomatoes, finely chopped
1 can (2¼ ounces) sliced black olives, drained and chopped
1 bag (10 ounces) tortilla chips
    Fresh cilantro for garnish

Place chicken in small bowl. Sprinkle with 3 tablespoons lime juice, garlic, salt
and pepper; mix well. Set aside. Combine beans, ½ cup sour cream,
2½ tablespoons taco seasoning mix and picante sauce in medium bowl. Spread
bean mixture in bottom of shallow 2-quart casserole dish. Combine avocado
and remaining 1 tablespoon lime juice in small bowl; sprinkle over bean
mixture. Combine remaining 1 cup sour cream and 2½ tablespoons taco
seasoning mix in small bowl; set aside. Heat oil in large skillet over high heat
until hot; add chicken in single layer. *Do not stir.* Cook about 2 minutes or until
chicken is brown on bottom. Turn chicken and cook until other side is brown
and no liquid remains. Break chicken into separate pieces with fork.

continued on page 32

Festive Chicken Dip

Festive Chicken Dip, continued

Layer chicken, sour cream mixture, cheese, onion and tomatoes over avocado mixture. Top with olives. Refrigerate until completely chilled. Serve with chips. Garnish with cilantro.   *Makes 2 quarts dip (about 30 appetizers)*

NUTRIENTS PER SERVING			
Calories	158	Fat	9 g
Cholesterol	20 mg	Sodium	331 mg

Favorite recipe from **National Broiler Council**

PHILLY® FREE® Salsa Dip

1 package (8 ounces) PHILADELPHIA BRAND® FREE® Fat
  Free Cream Cheese, softened
½ cup salsa

BEAT cream cheese with electric mixer on medium speed until well blended.

ADD salsa, mixing until blended. Refrigerate.

SERVE with assorted cut-up vegetables or lowfat tortilla chips.

Makes 12 servings (1½ cups)

Prep time: 5 minutes

NUTRIENTS PER SERVING			
(2 tablespoons)			
Calories	20	Fat	0 g
Cholesterol	5 mg	Sodium	140 mg

Chunky Hawaiian Spread

1 package (3 ounces) light cream cheese, softened
½ cup fat free or light sour cream
1 can (8 ounces) DOLE® Crushed Pineapple, well-drained
¼ cup mango chutney*
  Low fat crackers

• **Beat** cream cheese, sour cream, pineapple and chutney in bowl until blended. Cover and chill 1 hour or overnight. Serve with crackers. Refrigerate any leftover spread in airtight container for up to one week. *Makes 2½ cups*

*If there are large pieces of fruit in chutney, cut into small pieces.

NUTRIENTS PER SERVING			
(1 tablespoon)			
Calories	21	Fat	1 g
Cholesterol	1 mg	Sodium	23 mg

Lemon Dill Seafood Spread

2 packages (8 ounces each) light cream cheese, at room temperature
½ cup bottled lemon butter-dill cooking sauce
½ cup thinly sliced green onions
½ teaspoon lemon pepper seasoning
16 ounces surimi seafood, crab- or lobster-flavored, flake- or coarsely chopped chunk-style, drained

Blend cream cheese, cooking sauce, green onions and lemon pepper seasoning
in electric mixer or by hand. Stir in surimi seafood; press mixture into a 4-cup
mold lined with plastic wrap. Cover and refrigerate several hours or overnight.
Unmold on serving platter and garnish, if desired, with fresh dill or other fresh
herbs. Serve with crackers or melba toast.   *Makes 4 cups*

NUTRIENTS PER SERVING		
(1 tablespoon)		
Calories	32	Fat	2 g
Cholesterol	7 mg	Sodium	100 mg

Favorite recipe from **National Fisheries Institute**

Light and Zippy Dip

1   cup low fat cottage cheese
⅓   cup HEINZ® Chili Sauce
2   green onions, thinly sliced, including tops
1   teaspoon prepared horseradish
⅛   teaspoon ground red pepper*
     Crisp raw vegetables

Combine cottage cheese and chili sauce in food processor or blender. Process
until smooth, scraping sides. Stir in onions, horseradish and red pepper. Cover;
chill to blend flavors. Serve with vegetables.   *Makes about 1½ cups*

*Substitute 1/4 teaspoon black pepper for ground red pepper.

NUTRIENTS PER SERVING		
(2 tablespoons)		
Calories	22	Fat	<1 g
Cholesterol	1 mg	Sodium	176 mg

35

Five-Layered Mexican Dip

½ cup low fat sour cream
½ cup GUILTLESS GOURMET® Salsa (mild, medium or hot)
1 jar (12.5 ounces) GUILTLESS GOURMET® Bean Dip (Black or
    Pinto, mild or spicy)
2 cups shredded lettuce
½ cup chopped tomato
¼ cup (1 ounce) shredded sharp Cheddar cheese
    Chopped fresh cilantro and cilantro sprigs (optional)
1 large bag (7 ounces) GUILTLESS GOURMET® Baked Tortilla
    Chips (yellow, white or blue corn)

Mix together sour cream and salsa in small bowl. Spread bean dip in shallow glass bowl. Top with sour cream-salsa mixture, spreading to cover bean dip.* Just before serving, top with lettuce, tomato and cheese. Garnish with cilantro, if desired. Serve with tortilla chips.   *Makes 8 servings*

*Dip may be prepared to this point; cover and refrigerate up to 24 hours.

NUTRIENTS PER SERVING			
(⅔ cup dip and 20 chips)			
Calories	199	Fat	3 g
Cholesterol	8 mg	Sodium	425 mg

Five-Layered Mexican Dip

Fresh Tomato Pasta Soup

1   tablespoon olive oil
½   cup chopped onion
1   clove garlic, minced
3   pounds fresh tomatoes, coarsely chopped
3   cups fat-free reduced-sodium chicken broth
1   tablespoon minced fresh basil
1   tablespoon minced fresh marjoram
1   tablespoon minced fresh oregano
1   teaspoon fennel seed
½   teaspoon ground black pepper
¾   cup uncooked rosamarina or other small pasta
½   cup (2 ounces) shredded part-skim mozzarella cheese

1. Heat oil in large saucepan over medium heat. Add onion and garlic; cook and stir until onion is tender. Add tomatoes, broth, basil, marjoram, oregano, fennel seed and black pepper.

2. Bring to a boil; reduce heat. Cover; simmer 25 minutes. Remove from heat; cool slightly.

3. Puree tomato mixture in food processor or blender in batches. Return to saucepan; bring to a boil. Add pasta; cook 7 to 9 minutes or until tender. Transfer to serving bowls. Sprinkle with mozzarella. Garnish with marjoram sprigs, if desired.   *Makes 8 (¾-cup) servings*

NUTRIENTS PER SERVING			
Calories	116	Fat	4 g
Cholesterol	4 mg	Sodium	62 mg

Fresh Tomato Pasta Soup

Onion Soup with Crouton Crust

ONION SOUP

1	tablespoon vegetable oil
3	pounds large yellow onions, halved and thinly sliced (about 9 cups)
3	tablespoons all-purpose flour
⅔	cup apple brandy or water
5	cups low sodium beef stock or broth
2⅓	cups low sodium chicken stock or broth
1	tablespoon snipped fresh thyme leaves or 1 teaspoon dried thyme
1	teaspoon freshly ground black pepper
¼	teaspoon salt

CROUTON CRUST

8	slices (½ inch thick) whole wheat or white French bread
¾	cup (3 ounces) shredded ALPINE LACE® Reduced Fat Swiss Cheese

1. To make the Onion Soup: Spray a 6-quart Dutch oven or stockpot with nonstick cooking spray. Add the oil and heat over medium-high heat.

2. Add the onions and cook, stirring occasionally, for about 10 minutes or until browned and caramelized. Stir in the flour, then the brandy. Bring to a boil.

3. Add both of the stocks, the thyme, pepper and salt. Return to a boil, then reduce the heat to low and simmer, uncovered, for 30 minutes.

4. While the soup simmers, make the Crouton Crust: Preheat the broiler. Place the bread slices on a baking sheet and broil until nicely browned on both sides. Remove the bread slices from the baking sheet and set aside.

continued on page 42

Onion Soup with Crouton Crust

Onion Soup with Crouton Crust, continued

5. Place 8 ovenproof soup bowls on the baking sheet. Ladle the soup into the bowls and top each with a crouton. Sprinkle crouton and soup with the cheese. Broil 6 inches from the heat for 1 to 2 minutes or until cheese is melted and bubbly. *Makes 8 first-course servings (1 cup each)*

NUTRIENTS PER SERVING			
Calories	273	Fat	5 g
Cholesterol	10 mg	Sodium	366 mg

Dilled Vichyssoise

1 cup chopped leeks
1 large potato, peeled and cubed
¼ cup finely chopped green onions
2 cloves garlic, minced
2 teaspoons sugar
3 cups chicken broth
1 cup water
¾ cup 2% milk
2 tablespoons fresh dill, chopped finely

Place leeks, potato, green onions, garlic and sugar in large saucepan. Add chicken broth and water; simmer over medium heat 15 to 20 minutes or until potatoes are very tender. Remove from heat; puree soup in food processor or blender in batches. Stir in milk. Cover and refrigerate at least 3 hours before serving. *Makes 6 servings*

NUTRIENTS PER SERVING			
Calories	75	Fat	1 g
Cholesterol	3 mg	Sodium	154 mg

Favorite recipe from **The Sugar Association, Inc.**

Country Cream of Chicken Chowder

¼ cup CRISCO® Savory Seasonings Roasted Garlic Flavor oil
¼ cup finely chopped onion
¼ cup all-purpose flour
4 cups chicken broth
2 cups skim milk
1 bay leaf
3 cups frozen hash brown potatoes
1 package (10 ounces) frozen whole kernel corn
1 package (10 ounces) frozen cut green beans
1 package (10 ounces) frozen peas
1 package (10 ounces) frozen sliced carrots
1½ cups finely chopped cooked chicken
⅛ teaspoon pepper
2 tablespoons chopped fresh parsley or chives

1. Heat oil in large saucepan on medium heat. Add onion. Cook and stir until tender. Stir in flour. Cook until bubbly. Gradually stir in broth and milk. Cook and stir until mixture is bubbly and slightly thickened. Add bay leaf.

2. Add potatoes, corn, beans, peas and carrots. Increase heat to medium-high. Bring mixture back to a boil. Reduce heat to low. Simmer 5 minutes or until beans are tender. Stir in chicken and pepper. Heat thoroughly. Remove bay leaf. Serve sprinkled with parsley. *Makes 10 servings*

NUTRIENTS PER SERVING			
Calories	220	Fat	7 g
Cholesterol	20 mg	Sodium	685 mg

SMUCKER'S® Chilled Berry Soup

½ cup SMUCKER'S® Strawberry Jelly
3 cups fresh blueberries
2 cups fresh raspberries
  Juice of 1 lemon
1½ cups water, divided
1 teaspoon cornstarch dissolved in 2 tablespoons cold water
1 quart fresh strawberries, cleaned and sliced
1 cup plain nonfat yogurt or sour cream

In a large saucepan, combine the Smucker's® Strawberry Jelly with the blueberries, raspberries, lemon juice and 1 cup of the water. Bring to a boil; simmer about 5 minutes until the blueberries begin to lose some of their juice. Stir in the cornstarch dissolved in cold water; cook until slightly thickened, about 3 more minutes. Add the remaining ½ cup of water. Cool, then refrigerate the berry mixture until thoroughly chilled.

Place the chilled berry mixture in a blender or food processor. Blend on low speed for 5 minutes. Combine the puréed berry soup with the sliced strawberries. Spoon into serving bowls; stir a few tablespoons of yogurt or sour cream into each serving. *Makes 6 (1-cup) servings*

Prep time: 20 minutes
Chill time: 2 hours or longer

NUTRIENTS PER SERVING			
Calories	183	Fat	1 g
Cholesterol	1 mg	Sodium	38 mg

Hearty Tortilla Chip Soup

1 cup chopped onion

¾ cup finely chopped carrots

1 clove garlic, minced

6 ounces GUILTLESS GOURMET® Unsalted or Blue Corn Baked
Tortilla Chips, divided

3 cans (14½ ounces each) low sodium chicken broth, defatted

2 cups water

½ cup *each* GUILTLESS GOURMET® Roasted Red Pepper and
Green Tomatillo Salsas

1 can (6 ounces) low sodium tomato paste

1 cup (4 ounces) shredded low fat Monterey Jack cheese

Microwave Directions: Combine onion, carrots and garlic in 3-quart microwave-safe casserole. Cover with vented plastic wrap or lid; microwave on HIGH (100% power) 7 minutes or until vegetables are tender. Finely crush half the tortilla chips. Add crushed chips, broth, water, salsas and tomato paste; stir well. Cover; microwave on HIGH 6 minutes or until soup bubbles. Microwave on MEDIUM (50% power) 5 minutes. To serve, divide remaining tortilla chips and half the cheese among 6 individual soup bowls. Ladle soup over cheese and chips, dividing evenly. Sprinkle with remaining cheese. *Makes 8 servings*

Stove Top Directions: Bring 2 tablespoons broth to a boil in 3-quart saucepan over medium-high heat. Add onion, carrots and garlic; cook and stir about 5 minutes until vegetables are tender. Finely crush half the tortilla chips. Add crushed chips, remaining broth, water, salsas and tomato paste; stir well. Cook over medium heat until soup comes to a boil. Reduce heat to low; simmer 5 minutes. Serve as directed above.

NUTRIENTS PER SERVING			
Calories	180	Fat	4 g
Cholesterol	10 mg	Sodium	337 mg

Hearty Tortilla Chip Soup

Slimming Chocoberry Splash

Crushed ice
¾ cup cold skim milk
¼ cup sliced fresh strawberries
2 tablespoons HERSHEY'S Syrup
2 tablespoons vanilla ice milk
2 tablespoons club soda

Fill two tall glasses with crushed ice. In blender container, place all remaining ingredients except club soda. Cover; blend until smooth. Pour into glasses over crushed ice; add club soda. Serve immediately. Garnish as desired.

Makes 2 (6-ounce) servings

Variations: Substitute any of the following for strawberries: ⅓ cup drained canned peach slices; 3 tablespoons frozen raspberries; 2 pineapple slices *or* ¼ cup drained crushed canned pineapple.

NUTRIENTS PER SERVING			
Calories	100	Fat	1 g
Cholesterol	5 mg	Sodium	70 mg

Pineapple-Mint Lemonade

1 cup sugar
⅔ cup water*
1 can (46 ounces) DOLE® Pineapple Juice
1 cup lemon juice
⅓ cup chopped fresh mint
   Fresh mint sprigs (optional)

• **Combine** sugar and water in large saucepan; bring to boil. Boil 1 minute; remove from heat.

• **Stir** in pineapple juice, lemon juice and chopped mint; let stand 15 minutes.

• **Strain** lemonade into large pitcher; discard chopped mint. Serve over ice cubes in tall glasses. Garnish with mint sprigs. *Makes 8 servings*

Prep time: 15 minutes
Cook/Stand time: 20 minutes

*For less tart lemonade, use 1 cup water instead of ⅔ cup.

Summer Spritzer: Combine 2 cups Pineapple-Mint Lemonade with 2 cups mineral or sparkling water. Serve over ice. Makes 4 servings.

NUTRIENTS PER SERVING			
Calories	204	Fat	0 g
Cholesterol	0 mg	Sodium	9 mg

Clockwise from top right: Peach-Melon Cooler (page 52), Pineapple-Mint Lemonade and DOLE® Juice Spritzer (page 52)

Peach-Melon Cooler

3 cups cubed DOLE® Cantaloupe
5 cups DOLE® Orchard Peach Juice or Pineapple Orange Juice,
   divided

• **Place** melon and 1 cup juice in blender or food processor container; blend until smooth.

• **Combine** melon mixture and remaining juice in large pitcher. Chill 1 hour before serving.   *Makes 7 servings*

Prep time: 10 minutes
Chill time: 1 hour

NUTRIENTS PER SERVING			
Calories	124	Fat	0 g
Cholesterol	0 mg	Sodium	28 mg

DOLE® Juice Spritzer

½ cup DOLE® Pine-Passion-Banana Juice or other DOLE® Juice
½ cup mineral or sparkling water or club soda
   Strawberry or sliced fresh fruit (optional)

• **Pour** juice and mineral water over ice cubes in large glass. Garnish with fruit.
                                Makes 1 serving

Prep time: 5 minutes

NUTRIENTS PER SERVING			
Calories	70	Fat	0 g
Cholesterol	0 mg	Sodium	3 mg

Easy Chocolate Pudding Milk Shake

3 cups cold skim milk
1 package (4-serving size) JELL-O® Chocolate Flavor Fat Free
      Sugar Free Instant Reduced Calorie Pudding & Pie Filling
3 scoops (about 1½ cups) vanilla frozen lowfat yogurt

Pour cold milk into blender container. Add pudding mix and frozen yogurt; cover. Blend on high speed 15 seconds or until smooth.

Serve at once or refrigerate and stir before serving. (Mixture thickens as it stands. Thin with additional milk, if desired.)

Makes about 5 (1-cup) servings

NUTRIENTS PER SERVING			
Calories	160	Fat	2 g
Cholesterol	20 mg	Sodium	330 mg

Pineberry Smoothie

1 ripe DOLE® Banana, quartered
1 cup DOLE® Pineapple Juice
½ cup nonfat vanilla or plain yogurt
½ cup fresh or frozen strawberries, raspberries or blueberries

• **Combine** all ingredients in blender or food processor container. Blend until thick and smooth. Serve immediately.

Makes 2 servings

Prep time: 5 minutes

NUTRIENTS PER SERVING			
Calories	174	Fat	0 g
Cholesterol	1 mg	Sodium	37 mg

Hot Cocoa with Cinnamon

3 tablespoons sugar
3 tablespoons HERSHEY'S Cocoa
½ cup hot water
1 (3-inch) stick cinnamon
3 cups skim milk
½ teaspoon vanilla extract

In medium saucepan, stir together sugar and cocoa; gradually stir in water. Add cinnamon. Cook over medium heat, stirring constantly, until mixture boils; boil and stir 1 minute. Immediately stir in milk; continue cooking and stirring until mixture is hot. *Do not boil.* Remove from heat; discard cinnamon stick. Stir in vanilla. Beat with rotary beater or whisk until foamy. Serve immediately.

Makes 4 (7-ounce) servings

NUTRIENTS PER SERVING			
Calories	120	Fat	1 g
Cholesterol	5 mg	Sodium	95 mg

Hot Cocoa with Cinnamon

Breakfast & Brunch

• • • • • • • • • • •

Black Bean Pancakes & Salsa

1 cup GUILTLESS GOURMET® Black Bean Dip (mild or spicy)
2 egg whites
½ cup unbleached all-purpose flour
½ cup skim milk
1 tablespoon canola oil
Nonstick cooking spray
4 ounces fat free sour cream
½ cup GUILTLESS GOURMET® Salsa (mild, medium or hot)
Yellow tomatoes and fresh mint leaves (optional)

For pancake batter, place bean dip, egg whites, flour, milk and oil in blender or food processor; blend until smooth. Refrigerate 2 hours or overnight.

Preheat oven to 350°F. Coat large nonstick skillet with cooking spray; heat over medium heat until hot. For each pancake, spoon 2 tablespoons batter into skillet; cook until bubbles form and break on pancake surface. Turn pancakes over; cook until lightly browned on other side. Place on baking sheet; keep warm in oven. Repeat to make 16 small pancakes. (If batter becomes too thick, thin with more milk.) Serve hot with sour cream and salsa. Garnish with tomatoes and mint, if desired.

Makes 4 servings

NUTRIENTS PER SERVING			
(4 pancakes, 1 ounce sour cream and 2 tablespoons salsa)			
Calories	192	Fat	4 g
Cholesterol	0 mg	Sodium	403 mg

Black Bean Pancakes & Salsa

PB & J French Toast

¼ cup blueberry preserves, or any flavor
6 slices whole wheat bread, divided
¼ cup creamy peanut butter
½ cup EGG BEATERS® Healthy Real Egg Product
¼ cup skim milk
2 tablespoons FLEISCHMANN'S® Margarine
1 large banana, sliced
1 tablespoon honey
1 tablespoon orange juice
1 tablespoon PLANTER'S® Dry Roasted Unsalted Peanuts,
   chopped
   Low fat vanilla yogurt (optional)

Spread preserves evenly over 3 bread slices. Spread peanut butter evenly over remaining bread slices. Press preserves and peanut butter slices together to form 3 sandwiches; cut each diagonally in half. In shallow bowl, combine Egg Beaters® and milk. In large nonstick griddle or skillet, over medium-high heat, melt margarine. Dip each sandwich in egg mixture to coat; transfer to griddle. Cook sandwiches for 2 minutes on each side or until golden. Keep warm.

In small bowl, combine banana slices, honey, orange juice and peanuts. Arrange sandwiches on platter; top with banana mixture. Serve warm with a dollop of yogurt, if desired.   *Makes 6 servings*

Prep time: 25 minutes
Cook time: 10 minutes

NUTRIENTS PER SERVING			
Calories	242	Fat	11 g
Cholesterol	1 mg	Sodium	262 mg

PB & J French Toast

Silver Dollar Pancakes with Mixed Berry Topping

1¼ cups all-purpose flour
2 tablespoons sugar
2 teaspoons baking soda
1½ cups buttermilk
½ cup EGG BEATERS® Healthy Real Egg Product
3 tablespoons FLEISCHMANN'S® Margarine, melted, divided
Mixed Berry Topping (recipe follows)

In large bowl, combine flour, sugar and baking soda. Stir in buttermilk, Egg Beaters® and 2 tablespoons margarine just until blended.

Brush large nonstick griddle or skillet with some of remaining margarine; heat over medium-high heat. Using 1 heaping tablespoon batter for each pancake, spoon batter onto griddle. Cook until bubbly; turn and cook until lightly browned. Repeat with remaining batter, using remaining margarine as needed to make 28 pancakes. Serve hot with Mixed Berry Topping.

Makes 28 (2-inch) pancakes

Prep time: 20 minutes
Cook time: 20 minutes

Mixed Berry Topping: In medium saucepan, over medium-low heat, combine 1 (12-ounce) package frozen mixed berries,* thawed, ¼ cup honey and ½ teaspoon grated gingerroot (*or* ⅛ teaspoon ground ginger). Cook and stir just until hot and well blended. Serve over pancakes.

*3 cups mixed fresh berries may be substituted.

NUTRIENTS PER SERVING			
(4 pancakes, ¼ cup topping)			
Calories	228	Fat	6 g
Cholesterol	2 mg	Sodium	491 mg

Silver Dollar Pancakes with Mixed Berry Topping

Sunrise Pizza

2   small DOLE® Bananas, peeled
4   frozen waffles
¼   cup lowfat whipped cream cheese
1   can (11 ounces) DOLE® Mandarin Orange Segments, drained
2   teaspoons honey
    Dash ground cinnamon
    Fresh berry garnish

• **Thinly** slice bananas on diagonal.

• **Prepare** waffles according to package directions.

• **Spread** waffle with cream cheese. Arrange banana slices on top, overlapping.

• **Arrange** orange segments in center of each pizza. Drizzle with honey.
Sprinkle with cinnamon. Top each pizza with berries.   *Makes 4 servings*

Prep time: 15 minutes

NUTRIENTS PER SERVING			
Calories	230	Fat	6 g
Sodium	281 mg	Cholesterol	53 mg

Golden Apple French Toast

1 Golden Delicious apple, cored and sliced
½ cup apple juice
1 large egg, beaten
¼ teaspoon vanilla extract
2 slices bread
1 teaspoon cornstarch
⅛ teaspoon salt
⅛ teaspoon ground cardamom
1 tablespoon cold water

1. In small saucepan, combine apple slices and apple juice; heat to a simmer. Cook until apple slices are tender but still retain their shape, about 8 minutes. Remove from heat and set aside while preparing French toast.

2. For French toast, in wide, shallow bowl, combine egg and vanilla. Dip bread slices in egg mixture to coat both sides. In nonstick skillet, cook bread slices until lightly browned on both sides. Remove French toast to serving plates. With slotted spoon, remove apple slices from saucepan and arrange on top of French toast. For syrup, combine cornstarch, salt, cardamom, and water; stir into reserved apple juice in saucepan. Bring mixture to a boil, stirring constantly; cook until thickened and clear. Spoon syrup over apple slices and French toast and serve.

Makes 2 servings

NUTRIENTS PER SERVING			
Calories	198	Fat	4 g
Cholesterol	131 mg	Sodium	243 mg

Favorite recipe from **Washington Apple Commission**

Spicy Mexican Frittata

1   jalapeño pepper
1   clove garlic
1   medium tomato, peeled, halved, seeded and quartered
½   teaspoon ground coriander
½   teaspoon chili powder
½   cup chopped onion
1   cup frozen corn
6   egg whites
2   eggs
¼   cup skim milk
¼   teaspoon salt
¼   teaspoon black pepper
¼   cup (1 ounce) shredded part-skim farmer or mozzarella
      cheese

Add jalapeño pepper and garlic to food processor or blender. Process until finely chopped. Add tomato, coriander and chili powder. Cover; process until tomato is almost smooth.

Spray large skillet with nonstick cooking spray; heat skillet over medium heat. Cook and stir onion in hot skillet until tender. Stir in tomato mixture and corn. Cook 3 to 4 minutes or until liquid is almost evaporated, stirring occasionally.

Combine egg whites, eggs, milk, salt and black pepper in medium bowl. Add egg mixture all at once to skillet. Cook, without stirring, 2 minutes until eggs begin to set. Run large spoon around edge of skillet, lifting eggs for even cooking. Remove skillet from heat when eggs are almost set but surface is still moist. Sprinkle with cheese. Cover; let stand 3 to 4 minutes or until surface is set and cheese melts. Cut into wedges.   *Makes 4 servings*

NUTRIENTS PER SERVING			
Calories	129	Fat	3 g
Cholesterol	108 mg	Sodium	371 mg

Spicy Mexican Frittata

64

Western Omelet

½   cup finely chopped red or green bell pepper
⅓   cup cubed cooked potato
2   slices turkey bacon, diced
¼   teaspoon dried oregano leaves
2   teaspoons FLEISCHMANN'S® Margarine, divided
1   cup EGG BEATERS® Healthy Real Egg Product
    Fresh oregano sprig, for garnish

In 8-inch nonstick skillet, over medium heat, sauté bell pepper, potato, turkey bacon and dried oregano in 1 teaspoon margarine until tender.* Remove from skillet; keep warm.

In same skillet, over medium heat, melt remaining margarine. Pour Egg Beaters® into skillet. Cook, lifting edges to allow uncooked portion to flow underneath. When almost set, spoon vegetable mixture over half of omelet. Fold other half over vegetable mixture; slide onto serving plate. Garnish with fresh oregano.   *Makes 2 servings*

Prep time: 15 minutes
Cook time: 10 minutes

*For frittata, sauté vegetables and turkey bacon in 2 teaspoons margarine. Pour Egg Beaters® evenly into skillet over prepared vegetables. Cook without stirring for 4 to 5 minutes or until cooked on bottom and almost set on top. Carefully turn frittata; cook for 1 to 2 minutes more or until done. Slide onto serving platter; cut into wedges to serve.

NUTRIENTS PER SERVING			
Calories	147	Fat	6 g
Cholesterol	10 mg	Sodium	384 mg

Eggs Santa Fe

2 eggs
½ cup GUILTLESS GOURMET® Black Bean Dip (mild or spicy)
¼ cup GUILTLESS GOURMET® Salsa (mild, medium or hot)
1 ounce (about 20) GUILTLESS GOURMET® Unsalted Baked
   Tortilla Chips
2 tablespoons low fat sour cream
1 teaspoon chopped fresh cilantro
   Fresh cilantro sprigs (optional)

To poach eggs, bring water to a boil in small skillet over high heat; reduce heat to medium-low and maintain a simmer. Gently break eggs into water, being careful not to break yolks. Cover and simmer 5 minutes or until desired firmness.

Meanwhile, place bean dip in small microwave-safe bowl or small saucepan. Microwave bean dip on HIGH (100% power) 2 to 3 minutes or heat over medium heat until warm. To serve, spread ¼ cup warm bean dip in center of serving plate; top with 1 poached egg and 2 tablespoons salsa. Arrange 10 tortilla chips around egg. Dollop with 1 tablespoon sour cream and sprinkle with ½ teaspoon chopped cilantro. Repeat with remaining ingredients. Garnish with cilantro sprigs, if desired. *Makes 2 servings*

NUTRIENTS PER SERVING			
Calories	217	Fat	6 g
Cholesterol	218 mg	Sodium	430 mg

68

Asparagus-Swiss Soufflé

¼ cup unsalted butter substitute
½ cup chopped yellow onion
¼ cup all-purpose flour
½ teaspoon salt
¼ teaspoon cayenne pepper
1 cup 2% low fat milk
1 cup (4 ounces) shredded ALPINE LACE® Reduced Fat
    Swiss Cheese
1 cup egg substitute or 4 large eggs
1 cup coarsely chopped fresh asparagus pieces, cooked or
    frozen asparagus pieces, thawed and drained
3 large egg whites

1. Preheat the oven to 325°F. Spray a 1½-quart soufflé dish with nonstick cooking spray. In a large saucepan, melt the butter over medium heat, add the onion and sauté for 5 minutes or until soft. Stir in the flour, salt and pepper and cook for 2 minutes or until bubbly. Add the milk and cook, stirring constantly, for 5 minutes or until the sauce thickens. Add the cheese and stir until melted.

2. In a small bowl, whisk the egg substitute (or the whole eggs). Whisk in a little of the hot cheese sauce, then return this egg mixture to the saucepan and whisk until well blended. Remove from the heat and fold in the asparagus.

3. In a medium-size bowl, using an electric mixer set on high, beat the egg whites until stiff peaks form. Fold the hot cheese sauce into the whites, then spoon into the soufflé dish.

4. Place the soufflé on a baking sheet and bake for 50 minutes or until golden brown and puffy.   *Makes 8 servings*

NUTRIENTS PER SERVING			
Calories	164	Fat	9 g
Cholesterol	13 mg	Sodium	247 mg

Asparagus-Swiss Soufflé

Breakfast Burritos

4 slices LOUIS RICH® Turkey Bacon
2 flour tortillas (7 inches in diameter)
2 tablespoons shredded sharp Cheddar cheese
2 large egg whites
1 tablespoon chopped mild chilies
  Salsa or taco sauce (optional)
  Additional shredded sharp Cheddar cheese (optional)

Cook and stir turkey bacon in nonstick skillet over medium-high heat 8 to 10 minutes or until lightly browned.

Place 2 turkey bacon slices on each tortilla; sprinkle each tortilla with 1 tablespoon cheese.

Beat egg whites and chilies; add to hot skillet. Cook and stir about 2 minutes or until set.

Divide egg mixture between tortillas. Fold tortillas over filling. Top with salsa and additional cheese, if desired.   *Makes 2 burritos*

To keep burritos warm: Wrap filled burritos in foil and place in warm oven up to 30 minutes.

NUTRIENTS PER SERVING			
(1 burrito)			
Calories	220	Fat	9 g
Cholesterol	25 mg	Sodium	470 mg

Black Pepper Patties

1 package (about 1 pound) LOUIS RICH® Ground Turkey
1 teaspoon instant chicken bouillon
¼ teaspoon dried thyme leaves, crushed
1 teaspoon coarsely ground black pepper

SAUCE

1 large tomato, chopped
½ cup plain nonfat yogurt
1 tablespoon chopped fresh parsley

Mix turkey, bouillon and thyme in large bowl. Shape into four 4-inch patties. Sprinkle pepper on patties (about ⅛ teaspoon per side), lightly pressing pepper into turkey. Cook patties in nonstick skillet over medium heat about 12 minutes or until no longer pink, turning occasionally.

Meanwhile, mix sauce ingredients in small bowl. Serve cold sauce over turkey patties.   *Makes 4 servings*

NUTRIENTS PER SERVING			
(1 patty)			
Calories	190	Fat	8 g
Cholesterol	75 mg	Sodium	315 mg

73

Brunch Rice

1 teaspoon margarine
¾ cup shredded carrots
¾ cup diced green bell pepper
¾ cup (about 3 ounces) sliced fresh mushrooms
6 egg whites, beaten
2 eggs, beaten
½ cup skim milk
½ teaspoon salt
¼ teaspoon ground black pepper
3 cups cooked brown rice
½ cup (2 ounces) shredded Cheddar cheese
6 corn tortillas, warmed (optional)

Heat margarine in large skillet over medium-high heat until hot. Add carrots, green pepper and mushrooms; cook and stir 2 minutes. Combine egg whites, eggs, milk, salt and black pepper in small bowl. Reduce heat to medium and pour egg mixture over vegetables. Continue stirring 1½ to 2 minutes. Add rice and cheese; stir to gently separate grains. Cook 2 minutes. Serve immediately or spoon mixture into warmed corn tortillas.   *Makes 6 servings*

To Microwave: Heat margarine in 2- to 3-quart microproof baking dish. Add carrots, green pepper and mushrooms; cover and cook on HIGH (100% power) 4 minutes. Combine egg whites, eggs, milk, salt and black pepper in small bowl; pour over vegetables. Cook on HIGH 4 minutes, stirring with fork after each minute to cut cooked eggs into small pieces. Stir in rice and cheese; cook on HIGH about 1 minute or until thoroughly heated. Serve immediately or spoon mixture into warmed corn tortillas.

NUTRIENTS PER SERVING			
Calories	212	Fat	7 g
Cholesterol	79 mg	Sodium	353 mg

Favorite recipe from **USA Rice Council**

Brunch Rice

Brunch Quesadillas with Fruit Salsa

1 pint fresh strawberries, hulled and diced
1 fresh ripe Anjou pear, cored and diced
1 tablespoon chopped fresh cilantro
1 tablespoon honey
1 cup (4 ounces) SARGENTO® Preferred Light Fancy Supreme
   Shredded Mozzarella Cheese
4 flour tortillas (8 inches in diameter)
2 teaspoons light margarine, melted
2 tablespoons light sour cream

To make Fruit Salsa, combine strawberries, pear, cilantro and honey in medium bowl; set aside.

Sprinkle 2 tablespoons cheese on one half of each tortilla. Top with ⅓ cup Fruit Salsa (drain and discard any liquid from fruit) and another 2 tablespoons cheese. Fold tortillas in half. Brush top of each folded tortilla with some of the melted margarine.

Grill folded tortillas, greased sides down, in dry preheated skillet until light golden brown and crisp, about 2 minutes. Brush tops with remaining melted margarine; turn and brown other sides. Remove to serving plate or platter. Cut each tortilla in half. Serve with remaining Fruit Salsa. Garnish with sour cream. Serve immediately.   *Makes 4 servings*

NUTRIENTS PER SERVING			
Calories	278	Fat	9 g
Cholesterol	14 mg	Sodium	264 mg

Brunch Quesadillas with Fruit Salsa

Breakfast Risotto

4   cups cooked brown rice
2   cups (8 ounces) shredded GJETOST cheese
1   cup 1% low-fat milk
½   cup chopped walnuts or pecans (optional)
½   cup raisins
    Scant teaspoon cinnamon

In saucepan over medium heat, gently stir all ingredients together until hot and cheese is melted. Or, stir ingredients in microwave-safe pie plate and microwave on HIGH (100% power) 2½ minutes. Stir, then cook 1 additional minute if necessary.

Serve with green and red apple slices, strawberries or other fruit.

Makes 6 to 8 servings

NUTRIENTS PER SERVING			
Calories	279	Fat	9 g
Cholesterol	21 mg	Sodium	106 mg

Golden Apple Oatmeal

½   cup diced Golden Delicious apple
⅓   cup apple juice
⅓   cup water
¼   teaspoon salt (optional)
⅛   teaspoon ground cinnamon
⅛   teaspoon ground nutmeg
⅓   cup uncooked quick-cooking rolled oats

In small saucepan, combine apple, juice, water, salt (if desired), cinnamon, and nutmeg; heat to a boil. Stir in oats and cook 1 minute. Cover and let stand 2 minutes before serving.   *Makes 2 (½-cup) servings*

NUTRIENTS PER SERVING			
Calories	122	Fat	1 g
Cholesterol	0 mg	Sodium	661 mg

Favorite recipe from Washington Apple Commission

Breakfast S'mores

½ package KAVLI® Muesli crispbreads, cut in half crosswise
    while still wrapped
1 apple, thinly sliced
1 nectarine, thinly sliced
1 banana, thinly sliced
¼ cup natural-style peanut butter, with oil poured off
1 tablespoon honey
1 cup mini marshmallows

Arrange 9 crispbread pieces on baking sheet. (Reserve remaining 9 pieces for tops.)

Place sliced fruit on crispbreads in thin layers* (about ½ inch high).

Mix peanut butter with honey and place ¼ teaspoon on center of each fruit layer, circling it with 2 to 3 mini marshmallows.

Bake in 350°F oven 4 to 8 minutes or until marshmallows are melted. Place Kavli® lids on top and serve. *Makes 9 s'mores*

*Keep fruits separate for kids' s'mores; mix fruits for teens and adults.

NUTRIENTS PER SERVING			
Calories	109	Fat	4 g
Cholesterol	0 mg	Sodium	44 mg

Peach Gingerbread Muffins

2 cups all-purpose flour
2 teaspoons baking powder
1 teaspoon ground ginger
½ teaspoon salt
½ teaspoon ground cinnamon
¼ teaspoon ground cloves
½ cup sugar
½ cup MOTT'S® Chunky Apple Sauce
¼ cup MOTT'S® Apple Juice
¼ cup GRANDMA'S® Molasses
1 egg
2 tablespoons vegetable oil
1 (16-ounce) can peaches in juice, drained and chopped

1. Preheat oven to 400°F. Line 12 (2½-inch) muffin cups with paper liners or spray with nonstick cooking spray.

2. In large bowl, combine flour, baking powder, ginger, salt and spices.

3. In small bowl, combine sugar, apple sauce, apple juice, molasses, egg and oil.

4. Stir apple sauce mixture into flour mixture just until moistened. Fold in peaches.

5. Spoon evenly into prepared muffin cups.

6. Bake 20 minutes or until toothpick inserted in centers comes out clean. Immediately remove from pan; cool on wire rack 10 minutes. Serve warm or cool completely.

Makes 12 servings

NUTRIENTS PER SERVING			
Calories	190	Fat	3 g
Sodium	150 mg	Cholesterol	20 mg

Cranberry Poppy Seed Loaf

2½ cups all-purpose flour
¾ cup granulated sugar
2 tablespoons poppy seed
1 tablespoon DAVIS® Baking Powder
1 cup skim milk
⅓ cup FLEISCHMANN'S® Margarine, melted
¼ cup EGG BEATERS® Healthy Real Egg Product
1 teaspoon vanilla extract
2 teaspoons grated lemon peel
1 cup fresh or frozen cranberries, chopped
Powdered Sugar Glaze (recipe follows, optional)

In large bowl, combine flour, granulated sugar, poppy seed and baking powder; set aside.

In small bowl, combine milk, margarine, Egg Beaters®, vanilla and lemon peel. Stir milk mixture into flour mixture just until moistened. Stir in cranberries. Spread batter into greased 8½×4½×2¼-inch loaf pan. Bake at 350°F for 60 to 70 minutes or until toothpick inserted in center comes out clean. Cool in pan on wire rack. Drizzle with Powdered Sugar Glaze if desired.

Makes 12 servings

Powdered Sugar Glaze: In small bowl, combine 1 cup powdered sugar and 5 to 6 teaspoons water until smooth.

Prep time: 20 minutes
Cook time: 70 minutes

NUTRIENTS PER SERVING			
Calories	216	Fat	6 g
Cholesterol	0 mg	Sodium	172 mg

Cranberry Poppy Seed Loaf

Apple Sauce Cinnamon Rolls

ROLLS

4 cups all-purpose flour, divided
1 package active dry yeast
1 cup MOTT'S® Natural Apple Sauce, divided
½ cup skim milk
⅓ cup plus 2 tablespoons granulated sugar, divided
2 tablespoons margarine
½ teaspoon salt
1 egg, beaten lightly
2 teaspoons ground cinnamon

ICING

1 cup sifted powdered sugar
1 tablespoon skim milk
½ teaspoon vanilla extract

1. To prepare Rolls, in large bowl, combine 1½ cups flour and yeast. In small saucepan, combine ¾ cup apple sauce, ½ cup milk, 2 tablespoons granulated sugar, margarine and salt. Cook over medium heat, stirring frequently, until mixture reaches 120°F to 130°F and margarine is almost melted (milk will appear curdled). Add to flour mixture along with egg. Beat with electric mixer on low speed 30 seconds, scraping bowl frequently. Beat on high speed 3 minutes. Stir in 2¼ cups flour until soft dough forms.

2. Turn out dough onto lightly floured surface; flatten slightly. Knead 3 to 5 minutes or until smooth and elastic, adding remaining ¼ cup flour to prevent sticking if necessary. Shape dough into ball; place in large bowl sprayed with nonstick cooking spray. Turn dough over so that top is greased. Cover with towel; let rise in warm place about 1 hour or until doubled in bulk.

continued on page 86

Apple Sauce Cinnamon Rolls

Apple Sauce Cinnamon Rolls, continued

3. Spray two 8- or 9-inch round baking pans with nonstick cooking spray.

4. Punch down dough; turn out onto lightly floured surface. Cover with towel; let rest 10 minutes. Roll out dough into 12-inch square. Spread remaining ¼ cup apple sauce over dough to within ½ inch of edges. In small bowl, combine remaining ⅓ cup granulated sugar and cinnamon; sprinkle over apple sauce. Roll up dough jelly-roll style. Moisten edge with water; pinch to seal seam. Cut roll into 12 (1-inch) slices with sharp floured knife. Arrange 6 rolls ½ inch apart in each prepared pan. Cover with towel; let rise in warm place about 30 minutes or until nearly doubled in bulk.

5. Preheat oven to 375°F. Bake 20 to 25 minutes or until lightly browned. Cool on wire rack 5 minutes. Invert each pan onto serving plate.

6. To prepare Icing, in small bowl, combine powdered sugar, 1 tablespoon milk and vanilla until smooth. Drizzle over tops of rolls. Serve warm.

Makes 12 servings

NUTRIENTS PER SERVING			
Calories	260	Fat	3 g
Sodium	100 mg	Cholesterol	25 mg

Choco-Lowfat Muffins

1½ cups all-purpose flour
¾ cup granulated sugar
¼ cup HERSHEY₃S Cocoa or HERSHEY₃S European Style Cocoa
2 teaspoons baking powder
1 teaspoon baking soda
½ teaspoon salt
⅔ cup vanilla lowfat yogurt
⅔ cup skim milk
½ teaspoon vanilla extract
Powdered sugar (optional)

Heat oven to 400°F. Line 14 muffin cups (2½ inches in diameter) with paper bake cups. In medium bowl, stir together flour, granulated sugar, cocoa, baking powder, baking soda and salt; stir in yogurt, milk and vanilla just until combined. *(Do not beat.)* Fill muffin cups ⅔ full with batter.

Bake 15 to 20 minutes or until wooden pick inserted in centers comes out clean. Cool slightly in pans on wire racks. Remove from pans. Sprinkle powdered sugar over tops of muffins, if desired. Serve warm. Store, covered, at room temperature or freeze in airtight container for longer storage.

Makes 14 muffins

NUTRIENTS PER SERVING			
(1 muffin)			
Calories	100	Fat	1 g
Cholesterol	0 mg	Sodium	200 mg

Apricot Carrot Bread

1¾ cups all-purpose flour
1 teaspoon baking powder
¼ teaspoon baking soda
¼ teaspoon salt
½ cup granulated sugar
½ cup finely shredded carrots
½ cup MOTT'S® Natural Apple Sauce
1 egg, beaten lightly
2 tablespoons vegetable oil
⅓ cup dried apricots, snipped into small bits
½ cup powdered sugar
2 teaspoons MOTT'S® Apple Juice

1. Preheat oven to 350°F. Spray 8×4-inch loaf pan with nonstick cooking spray.

2. In large bowl, combine flour, baking powder, baking soda and salt.

3. In small bowl, combine granulated sugar, carrots, apple sauce, egg and oil.

4. Stir apple sauce mixture into flour mixture just until moistened. (Batter will be thick.) Fold in apricots. Spread batter into prepared pan.

5. Bake 45 to 50 minutes or until toothpick inserted in center comes out clean. Cool in pan 10 minutes. Invert onto wire rack; turn right side up. Cool completely. For best flavor, wrap loaf in plastic wrap or foil; store at room temperature overnight.

6. Just before serving, in small bowl, combine powdered sugar and apple juice until smooth. Drizzle over top of loaf. Cut into 12 slices. *Makes 12 servings*

NUTRIENTS PER SERVING			
Calories	160	Fat	3 g
Cholesterol	20 mg	Sodium	95 mg

Apricot Carrot Bread

Jelly Donut Muffins

1¼ cups nonfat milk
¼ cup Prune Purée (recipe follows) or prepared prune butter
1 egg
2 tablespoons vegetable oil
1 teaspoon vanilla
2 cups all-purpose flour
⅓ cup sugar
1 tablespoon baking powder
1 teaspoon ground cardamom or cinnamon
½ teaspoon salt
¼ cup strawberry jam

Preheat oven to 425°F. Coat twelve 2¾-inch (⅓-cup capacity) muffin cups with vegetable cooking spray. In large bowl, beat first five ingredients until well blended. In medium bowl, combine flour, sugar, baking powder, cardamom and salt. Add to milk mixture; mix just until blended. Spoon about half of batter into prepared muffin cups. Top each with 1 teaspoon jam and remaining batter, covering jam completely. Bake 15 to 20 minutes or until springy to the touch. Cool in pans 10 minutes. Remove to wire rack to cool slightly. Serve warm.

Makes 12 muffins

Prune Purée: Combine 1⅓ cups (8 ounces) pitted prunes and 6 tablespoons hot water in container of food processor or blender. Pulse on and off until prunes are finely chopped and smooth. Store leftovers in a covered container in the refrigerator for up to two months. Makes 1 cup.

NUTRIENTS PER SERVING			
(1 muffin)			
Calories	160	Fat	3 g
Cholesterol	20 mg	Sodium	280 mg

Favorite recipe from **California Prune Board**

Jelly Donut Muffins

Apple Sauce Coffee Ring

BREAD

1	package active dry yeast
⅓	cup plus 1 teaspoon granulated sugar, divided
¼	cup warm water (105° to 115°F)
½	cup skim milk
½	cup MOTT'S® Natural Apple Sauce
1	egg
2	tablespoons margarine, melted and cooled
1	teaspoon salt
1	teaspoon grated lemon peel
5	cups all-purpose flour
1	teaspoon skim milk

FILLING

1½	cups MOTT'S® Chunky Apple Sauce
½	cup raisins
⅓	cup firmly packed light brown sugar
1	teaspoon ground cinnamon

GLAZE

1	cup powdered sugar
2	tablespoons skim milk
1	teaspoon vanilla extract

1. To prepare Bread, in large bowl, sprinkle yeast and 1 teaspoon granulated sugar over warm water; stir until yeast dissolves. Let stand 5 minutes or until mixture is bubbly. Stir in ½ cup milk, ½ cup apple sauce, remaining ⅓ cup granulated sugar, egg, margarine, salt and lemon peel.

continued on page 94

Apple Sauce Coffee Ring

Apple Sauce Coffee Ring, continued

2. Stir in flour, 1 cup at a time, until soft dough forms. Turn out dough onto floured surface; flatten slightly. Knead 5 minutes or until smooth and elastic, adding any remaining flour to prevent sticking if necessary. Shape dough into ball; place in large bowl sprayed with nonstick cooking spray. Turn dough over so that top is greased. Cover with damp towel; let rise in warm place 1 hour or until doubled in bulk.

3. Punch down dough. Roll out dough on floured surface into 15-inch square. Spray baking sheet with nonstick cooking spray.

4. **To prepare Filling,** in small bowl, combine 1½ cups chunky apple sauce, raisins, brown sugar and cinnamon. Spread filling over dough to within ½ inch of edges. Roll up dough jelly-roll style. Moisten edge with water; pinch to seal seam. Moisten ends of dough with water; bring together to form ring. Pinch to seal seam. Place on prepared baking sheet. Make ⅛-inch-deep cuts across width of dough at 2-inch intervals around ring.

5. Let dough rise in warm place, uncovered, 30 minutes.

6. Preheat oven to 350°F. Brush top lightly with 1 teaspoon milk.

7. Bake 45 to 50 minutes or until lightly browned and ring sounds hollow when tapped. Remove from baking sheet; cool completely on wire rack.

8. **To prepare Glaze,** in small bowl, combine powdered sugar, 2 tablespoons milk and vanilla until smooth. Drizzle over top of ring. Cut into 24 slices.

Makes 24 servings

NUTRIENTS PER SERVING			
Calories	170	Fat	2 g
Sodium	110 mg	Cholesterol	10 mg

Chili-Cheese Cornbread

1 cup yellow cornmeal
⅔ cup all-purpose flour
2 teaspoons baking powder
½ teaspoon salt
¾ cup nonfat sour cream alternative
2 egg whites
1 egg
¼ cup CRISCO® Oil
1½ cups finely chopped fat free process cheese product slices
    (¾ ounce each)
1 can (8¾ ounces) whole kernel corn, drained
1 can (4 ounces) chopped green chilies, drained

1. Heat oven to 400°F. Grease 9-inch square pan.

2. Combine cornmeal, flour, baking powder and salt in small bowl.

3. Combine "sour cream," egg whites, egg and oil in medium bowl. Stir well. Add cornmeal mixture, cheese, corn and chilies. Mix well. Pour into pan.

4. Bake at 400°F for 30 to 35 minutes or until toothpick inserted in center comes out clean. Cool 10 to 15 minutes. Cut into squares. Serve warm.

Makes 8 servings

NUTRIENTS PER SERVING			
Calories	255	Fat	8 g
Cholesterol	30 mg	Sodium	860 mg

Blueberry Muffins

1 cup fresh or thawed frozen blueberries
1¾ cups plus 1 tablespoon all-purpose flour, divided
2 teaspoons baking powder
1 teaspoon grated lemon peel
½ teaspoon salt
½ cup MOTT'S® Apple Sauce
½ cup sugar
1 whole egg
1 egg white
2 tablespoons vegetable oil
¼ cup skim milk

1. Preheat oven to 375°F. Line 12 (2½-inch) muffin cups with paper liners or spray with nonstick cooking spray.

2. In small bowl, toss blueberries with 1 tablespoon flour.

3. In large bowl, combine remaining 1¾ cups flour, baking powder, lemon peel and salt.

4. In another small bowl, combine apple sauce, sugar, whole egg, egg white and oil.

5. Stir apple sauce mixture into flour mixture alternately with milk. Mix just until moistened. Fold in blueberry mixture.

6. Spoon evenly into prepared muffin cups.

7. Bake 20 minutes or until toothpick inserted in centers comes out clean. Immediately remove from pan; cool on wire rack 10 minutes. Serve warm or cool completely.   *Makes 12 servings*

NUTRIENTS PER SERVING			
Calories	150	Fat	3 g
Sodium	150 mg	Cholesterol	20 mg

Blueberry Muffins

Oatmeal Apple Cranberry Scones

2 cups all-purpose flour
1 cup uncooked rolled oats
⅓ cup sugar
2 teaspoons baking powder
½ teaspoon salt
½ teaspoon baking soda
½ teaspoon ground cinnamon
¾ cup MOTT'S® Natural Apple Sauce, divided
2 tablespoons margarine
½ cup coarsely chopped cranberries
½ cup peeled, chopped apple
¼ cup skim milk
¼ cup plus 2 tablespoons honey, divided

1. Preheat oven to 425°F. Spray baking sheet with nonstick cooking spray. In large bowl, combine flour, oats, sugar, baking powder, salt, baking soda and cinnamon. Add ½ cup apple sauce and margarine; cut in with pastry blender or fork until mixture resembles coarse crumbs. Stir in cranberries and apple.

2. In small bowl, combine milk and ¼ cup honey. Add milk mixture to flour mixture; stir together until dough forms a ball. Turn out dough onto well-floured surface; knead 10 to 12 times. Pat into 8-inch circle. Place on baking sheet. Use tip of knife to score dough into 12 wedges.

3. In another small bowl, combine remaining ¼ cup apple sauce and 2 tablespoons honey. Brush mixture over top of dough.

4. Bake 12 to 15 minutes or until lightly browned. Immediately remove from baking sheet; cool on wire rack 10 minutes. Serve warm or cool completely. Cut into 12 wedges.

Makes 12 servings

NUTRIENTS PER SERVING			
Calories	170	Fat	2 g
Sodium	200 mg	Cholesterol	0 mg

Oatmeal Apple Cranberry Scones

Meats

Sweet and Spicy Pork Tenderloin

2 teaspoons dried tarragon leaves
½ teaspoon dried thyme leaves
⅛ to ½ teaspoon black pepper
¼ teaspoon ground red pepper
  Dash salt
1 pound pork tenderloin, trimmed and cut crosswise into
    ½-inch pieces
2 tablespoons margarine, melted
1½ tablespoons honey

In small bowl, combine tarragon, thyme, peppers and salt; blend well. Brush both sides of each pork tenderloin piece with margarine; sprinkle both sides with seasoning mixture. Arrange tenderloin pieces on broiler pan. Broil, 5 to 6 inches from heat source, for 2 minutes per side. Remove from broiler. Brush top side of each piece with honey. Broil for an additional minute. Place pork pieces on serving plate.

Makes 4 servings

NUTRIENTS PER SERVING			
Calories	219	Fat	10 g
Cholesterol	79 mg	Sodium	158 mg

Favorite recipe from **National Pork Producers Council**

Sweet and Spicy Pork Tenderloin

Mandarin Pork Stir-Fry

1½ cups DOLE® Mandarin Tangerine, Pineapple Orange or
   Pineapple Juice, divided
   Vegetable cooking spray
12 ounces lean pork tenderloin, chicken breast or turkey
   tenderloin, cut into thin strips
1 tablespoon finely chopped fresh ginger *or* ½ teaspoon ground
   ginger
2 cups DOLE® Shredded Carrots
½ cup chopped DOLE® Pitted Prunes or Chopped Dates
4 DOLE® Green Onions, cut into 1-inch pieces
2 tablespoons low-sodium soy sauce
1 teaspoon cornstarch

• **Heat** 2 tablespoons juice over medium-high heat in large nonstick skillet sprayed with vegetable cooking spray until juice bubbles.

• **Add** pork; cook and stir 3 minutes or until pork is no longer pink. Remove pork from skillet.

• **Heat** 3 more tablespoons juice in skillet; add carrots, prunes and green onions. Cook and stir 3 minutes.

• **Stir** soy sauce and cornstarch into remaining juice; add to carrot mixture. Stir in pork; cover and cook 2 minutes until heated through.   *Makes 4 servings*

Prep time: 15 minutes
Cook time: 15 minutes

NUTRIENTS PER SERVING			
Calories	225	Fat	4 g
Cholesterol	71 mg	Sodium	312 mg

Mandarin Pork Stir-Fry

Margarita Pork Kabobs

1 cup margarita drink mix *or* 1 cup lime juice, 4 teaspoons
      sugar and ½ teaspoon salt
1 teaspoon ground coriander
1 clove garlic, minced
1 pound pork tenderloin, cut into 1-inch cubes
2 tablespoons margarine, softened
2 teaspoons lime juice
1 tablespoon minced fresh parsley
⅛ teaspoon sugar
1 large green or red bell pepper, cut into 1-inch cubes
2 ears corn, cut into 8 pieces

Combine margarita mix, coriander and garlic in small bowl. Place pork cubes in large resealable plastic food storage bag; pour marinade over pork. Close bag securely; turn to coat. Marinate for at least 30 minutes. Combine margarine, lime juice, parsley and sugar in small bowl; set aside. Thread pork cubes onto four skewers, alternating with pieces of bell pepper and corn. (If using bamboo skewers, soak in water 20 to 30 minutes before using to prevent them from burning). Grill over hot coals for 15 to 20 minutes, basting with margarine mixture and turning frequently.

Makes 4 servings

NUTRIENTS PER SERVING			
Calories	298	Fat	9 g
Cholesterol	64 mg	Sodium	309 mg

Favorite recipe from **National Pork Producers Council**

Margarita Pork Kabobs

Stuffed Pork Tenderloin

2 teaspoons minced garlic
2 teaspoons snipped fresh rosemary leaves or ½ teaspoon dried
    rosemary
2 teaspoons snipped fresh thyme leaves or ½ teaspoon dried
    thyme
1 teaspoon salt
½ teaspoon freshly ground black pepper
1 boneless end-cut rolled pork loin with tenderloin attached
    (4 pounds), tied
1 tablespoon unsalted butter substitute
1 cup thin strips yellow onion
2 large tart apples, peeled, cored and thinly sliced (2 cups)
10 thin slices (½ ounce each) ALPINE LACE® Reduced Fat
    Swiss Cheese
1 cup apple cider or apple juice

1. Preheat the oven to 325°F. Fit a 13×9×3-inch baking pan with a rack. In a small bowl, combine the garlic, rosemary, thyme, salt and pepper. Untie and unroll the pork loin, laying it flat. Rub half of the spice mixture onto the pork.

2. In a medium-size skillet, melt the butter over medium-high heat. Add the onion and apples and sauté for 5 minutes or until soft. Spread this mixture evenly on the pork and cover with the cheese slices.

3. Starting from one of the widest ends, re-roll the pork, jelly-roll style. Tie the roast with cotton string at 1-inch intervals and rub the outside with the remaining spice mixture. Place the roast on the rack in the pan and pour the apple cider over it.

continued on page 108

Stuffed Pork Tenderloin

Stuffed Pork Tenderloin, continued

4. Roast, uncovered, basting frequently with the pan drippings, for 2 to 2½ hours or until an instant-read thermometer inserted in the thickest part registers 160°F. Let the roast stand for 15 minutes before slicing.

Makes 16 servings

NUTRIENTS PER SERVING			
(½-inch slice)			
Calories	190	Fat	10 g
Cholesterol	57 mg	Sodium	184 mg

Pork Tenderloin with Raisin Sauce

1	pound pork tenderloin, trimmed of visible fat
1	jar (12 ounces) HEINZ® Fat Free Beef Gravy
⅓	cup golden raisins
3	tablespoons apple jelly
	Dash pepper
1	tablespoon Dijon-style mustard

Cut pork crosswise into 8 pieces; pound each piece to ½-inch thickness. Spray skillet with nonstick cooking spray. Quickly brown pork in skillet, about 1 minute per side. Stir in gravy, raisins, jelly and pepper. Simmer 10 minutes or until pork is no longer pink, stirring sauce and turning pork occasionally. Remove pork. Add mustard to sauce, stirring until blended. Serve sauce over pork.

Makes 4 servings (about 1⅓ cups sauce)

NUTRIENTS PER SERVING			
Calories	232	Fat	3 g
Cholesterol	72 mg	Sodium	110 mg

Caribbean Jerk-Style Pork

¾ cup DOLE® Pineapple Juice, Pineapple Orange Juice or
   Mandarin Tangerine Juice, divided
1 tablespoon prepared yellow mustard
1 teaspoon dried thyme leaves, crushed
¼ teaspoon crushed red pepper
12 ounces boneless pork loin chops or chicken breasts, cut into
   strips
½ cup DOLE® Golden or Seedless Raisins
½ cup sliced DOLE® Green Onions
2 medium firm DOLE® Bananas, cut diagonally into
   ¼-inch slices
   Hot cooked rice or noodles (optional)

• **Stir** together ½ cup juice, mustard, thyme and red pepper in small bowl; set aside.

• **Place** pork in large, nonstick skillet sprayed with vegetable cooking spray. Cook and stir pork over medium-high heat 3 to 5 minutes or until pork is no longer pink. Remove pork from skillet.

• **Add** remaining ¼ cup juice to skillet; stir in raisins and green onions. Cook and stir 1 minute.

• **Stir** in pork and reserved mustard mixture; cover and cook 2 minutes or until heated through. Stir in bananas. Serve over hot rice.   *Makes 4 servings*

Prep time: 10 minutes
Cook time: 10 minutes

NUTRIENTS PER SERVING			
Calories	282	Fat	5 g
Cholesterol	79 mg	Sodium	111 mg

109

Pork with Sweet Hungarian Paprika

1 teaspoon olive oil, divided
1 onion, sliced
2 cloves garlic, minced
1 tomato, chopped
1 red bell pepper, chopped
1 large Anaheim *or* 1 medium green bell pepper, chopped
1 can (10½ ounces) fat-free reduced-sodium chicken broth, divided
2 tablespoons sweet Hungarian paprika
12 ounces pork tenderloin
3 tablespoons all-purpose flour
⅓ cup low-fat sour cream
6 cups cooked enriched egg noodles (6 ounces uncooked)
¼ cup minced parsley (optional)

1. Heat ½ teaspoon oil in medium saucepan over medium heat until hot. Add onion and garlic. Cook and stir 2 minutes. Add tomato, peppers, ½ cup chicken broth and paprika. Reduce heat to low; cover and simmer 5 minutes.

2. Cut pork crosswise into 8 slices. Pound pork to ¼-inch thickness using flat side of meat mallet or rolling pin. Heat remaining ½ teaspoon oil in nonstick skillet over medium heat until hot. Cook pork 1 minute on each side or until browned. Add onion mixture. Reduce heat to low; simmer 5 minutes. Whisk remaining chicken broth and flour in small bowl.

3. Remove pork from skillet. Stir flour mixture into liquid in skillet. Bring to a boil; remove from heat. Stir in sour cream. Serve over pork and noodles. Garnish with additional paprika and parsley, if desired.   *Makes 4 servings*

NUTRIENTS PER SERVING			
Calories	380	Fat	9 g
Cholesterol	110 mg	Sodium	96 mg

New Orleans Pork Gumbo

1 pound pork loin roast
  Nonstick cooking spray
1 tablespoon margarine
2 tablespoons all-purpose flour
1 cup water
1 can (16 ounces) stewed tomatoes, undrained
1 package (10 ounces) frozen cut okra
1 package (10 ounces) frozen succotash
1 beef bouillon cube
1 teaspoon hot pepper sauce
1 teaspoon coarsely ground black pepper
1 bay leaf

1. Cut pork into ½-inch cubes. Spray large Dutch oven with cooking spray. Heat over medium heat until hot. Add pork; cook and stir 4 minutes or until pork is browned. Remove pork from Dutch oven.

2. Add margarine to Dutch oven. Stir in flour. Cook and stir until roux is browned. Whisk in water. Add pork and remaining ingredients. Bring to a boil. Reduce heat to low and simmer 15 minutes. Remove bay leaf and discard.

Makes 4 servings

NUTRIENTS PER SERVING			
Calories	295	Fat	10 g
Cholesterol	45 mg	Sodium	602 mg

Tandoori Pork Sauté

Nutty Rice (recipe follows)
8 ounces lean pork, cut into 2×½-inch strips
½ cup sliced onion
1 clove garlic, minced
4 fresh California plums, halved, pitted and cut into thick
   wedges
1 cup plain low-fat yogurt
1 tablespoon all-purpose flour
1½ teaspoons grated fresh ginger
½ teaspoon ground turmeric
⅛ teaspoon ground black pepper
Additional plum wedges, orange sections and sliced green
   onions

Prepare Nutty Rice. Cook pork in nonstick skillet 2 minutes or until browned, turning occasionally. Transfer to platter. Add onion and garlic to skillet; cook 1 minute. Add plums; cook and stir 1 minute. Remove from heat and return pork to pan. Combine yogurt and flour; add to skillet. Stir in ginger, turmeric and pepper. Bring to a boil; reduce heat and simmer 10 minutes, stirring occasionally. Serve over Nutty Rice and surround with plum wedges, orange sections and green onions. *Makes 4 servings*

Nutty Rice: Bring 2 cups water to a boil in medium saucepan. Add ¾ cup brown rice and ¼ cup wheat berries. (Or, omit wheat berries and use 1 cup brown rice.) Return to a boil. Reduce heat to low; cover and simmer 40 to 45 minutes or until rice is tender and liquid is absorbed. Makes about 2 cups.

NUTRIENTS PER SERVING			
Calories	287	Fat	4 g
Cholesterol	44 mg	Sodium	73 mg

Favorite recipe from **California Tree Fruit Agreement**

Tandoori Pork Sauté

Potato and Pork Frittata

12 ounces (about 3 cups) frozen hash brown potatoes
1 teaspoon Cajun seasoning
4 egg whites
2 whole eggs
¼ cup 1% low fat milk
1 teaspoon dry mustard
¼ teaspoon coarsely ground black pepper
10 ounces (about 3 cups) frozen stir-fry vegetables
¾ cup chopped cooked lean pork
½ cup (2 ounces) shredded Cheddar cheese

1. Preheat oven to 400°F. Spray baking sheet with nonstick cooking spray. Spread potatoes on baking sheet; sprinkle with Cajun seasoning. Bake 15 minutes or until hot. Remove from oven. Reduce oven temperature to 350°F.

2. Beat egg whites, eggs, milk, mustard and pepper in small bowl. Place vegetables and ⅓ cup water in medium nonstick skillet. Cook over medium heat 5 minutes or until vegetables are crisp-tender; drain.

3. Add pork and potatoes to vegetables in skillet; stir lightly. Add egg mixture. Sprinkle with cheese. Cook over medium-low heat 5 minutes. Place skillet in 350°F oven and bake 5 minutes or until egg mixture is set and cheese is melted.   *Makes 4 servings*

NUTRIENTS PER SERVING			
Calories	251	Fat	7 g
Cholesterol	135 mg	Sodium	394 mg

Potato and Pork Frittata

Beef & Bean Burritos

Nonstick cooking spray
½ pound beef round steak, cut into ½-inch pieces
3 cloves garlic, minced
1 can (about 15 ounces) pinto beans, rinsed and drained
1 can (4 ounces) diced mild green chilies, drained
¼ cup finely chopped fresh cilantro
6 (6-inch) flour tortillas
½ cup (2 ounces) shredded reduced fat Cheddar cheese

1. Spray nonstick skillet with cooking spray; heat over medium heat until hot. Add steak and garlic; cook and stir 5 minutes or until steak is cooked to desired doneness.

2. Stir beans, chilies and cilantro into skillet; cook and stir 5 minutes or until heated through.

3. Spoon steak mixture evenly down center of each tortilla; sprinkle cheese evenly over each tortilla. Fold bottom end of tortilla over filling; roll to enclose. Garnish with salsa and nonfat sour cream, if desired. *Makes 6 servings*

NUTRIENTS PER SERVING			
Calories	278	Fat	7 g
Cholesterol	31 mg	Sodium	956 mg

Beef & Bean Burrito

Old-Fashioned Beef Stew

1 tablespoon CRISCO® Savory Seasonings Roasted Garlic Flavor oil
1¼ pounds boneless beef round steak, trimmed and cut into
    1-inch cubes
2¾ cups water, divided
1 teaspoon Worcestershire sauce
2 bay leaves
1 clove garlic, minced
½ teaspoon paprika
¼ teaspoon pepper
8 medium carrots, quartered
8 small potatoes, peeled and quartered
4 small onions, quartered
1 package (9 ounces) frozen cut green beans
1 tablespoon cornstarch
Salt (optional)

1. Heat oil in Dutch oven on medium-high heat. Add beef. Cook and stir until browned. Add 1½ cups water, Worcestershire sauce, bay leaves, garlic, paprika and pepper. Bring to a boil. Reduce heat to low. Cover and simmer 1 hour 15 minutes, stirring occasionally. Remove bay leaves.

2. Add carrots, potatoes and onions. Cover and simmer 30 to 45 minutes or until vegetables are almost tender. Add beans. Simmer 5 minutes or until tender. Remove from heat. Add 1 cup water to Dutch oven.

3. Combine remaining ¼ cup water and cornstarch in small bowl. Stir well. Stir into ingredients in Dutch oven. Return to low heat. Cook and stir until thickened. Season with salt, if desired. *Makes 8 servings*

NUTRIENTS PER SERVING			
Calories	290	Fat	8 g
Cholesterol	60 mg	Sodium	95 mg

Mighty Hero Sandwich

1 (16-ounce) round loaf sourdough bread
¼ cup balsamic vinegar
1 tablespoon olive oil
2 cloves garlic, minced
1 teaspoon dried oregano leaves
1 teaspoon dried parsley flakes
¼ teaspoon pepper
1 cup sliced fresh mushrooms
6 (¼-inch-thick) tomato slices
2 (¼-inch-thick) red onion slices, separated into rings
2 cups shredded zucchini
1 cup (4 ounces) HEALTHY CHOICE® Fat Free Mozzarella
   Shreds
4 ounces HEALTHY CHOICE® Deli Thin Sliced Bologna
4 ounces HEALTHY CHOICE® Deli Thin Oven Roasted
   Turkey Breast

Slice bread in half horizontally. Remove soft bread from inside each half, leaving ½-inch-thick shells; set shells aside. Reserve soft inside bread for another use.

Combine vinegar and next 5 ingredients in shallow dish; add mushrooms, tomato and onion. Let stand 15 minutes.

Drain vegetables, reserving marinade. Brush marinade inside bread shells. Layer half each of zucchini, mushroom mixture and cheese in bottom half of loaf; top with bologna. Repeat layers; top with turkey and top half of loaf. Wrap in plastic wrap; chill. To serve, unwrap loaf and cut into wedges.

Makes 8 servings

NUTRIENTS PER SERVING			
Calories	192	Fat	4 g
Cholesterol	16 mg	Sodium	591 mg

Beef Cubed Steaks Provençale

2 cloves garlic, minced
½ teaspoon dried basil leaves
¼ teaspoon black pepper
4 lean beef cubed steaks (about 4 ounces each)
1½ teaspoons olive oil
2 small zucchini, thinly sliced
6 cherry tomatoes, cut in half
1½ teaspoons grated Parmesan cheese
Salt (optional)

Combine garlic, basil and pepper; divide mixture in half. Press half of seasoning mixture evenly into both sides of beef cubed steaks; set aside. Heat oil and remaining seasoning mixture in large nonstick skillet over medium heat. Add zucchini; cook and stir 3 minutes. Add tomatoes; continue cooking 1 minute, stirring frequently. Remove zucchini mixture to platter; sprinkle with cheese and keep warm. Increase heat to medium-high. Add 2 steaks to same skillet; cook to desired doneness, 3 to 4 minutes, turning once. Repeat with remaining 2 steaks. Season steaks with salt, if desired. Serve with zucchini mixture; garnish as desired. *Makes 4 servings*

NUTRIENTS PER SERVING			
Calories	223	Fat	10 g
Cholesterol	81 mg	Sodium	60 mg

Favorite recipe from **National Cattlemen's Beef Association**

Beef Cubed Steak Provençale

Grilled Flank Steak with Horseradish Sauce

1 pound beef flank steak
2 tablespoons reduced-sodium soy sauce
1 tablespoon red wine vinegar
2 cloves garlic, minced
½ teaspoon pepper
1 cup nonfat sour cream
1 tablespoon prepared horseradish
1 tablespoon Dijon mustard
¼ cup finely chopped fresh parsley
½ teaspoon salt
6 sourdough rolls, split
6 romaine lettuce leaves

1. Place flank steak in large resealable plastic food storage bag. Add soy sauce, vinegar, garlic and pepper. Close bag securely; turn to coat. Marinate in refrigerator at least 1 hour.

2. Prepare grill or preheat broiler. Drain steak; discard marinade. Grill or broil over medium-high heat 5 minutes. Turn beef; grill 6 minutes for medium-rare or until desired doneness. Cover with foil; let stand 15 minutes. Thinly slice steak across grain.

3. Combine sour cream, horseradish, mustard, parsley and salt in small bowl until well blended. Spread rolls with horseradish sauce; layer with sliced steak and lettuce. Garnish with small pickles, if desired. *Makes 6 servings*

NUTRIENTS PER SERVING			
Calories	220	Fat	6 g
Cholesterol	35 mg	Sodium	542 mg

Grilled Flank Steak with Horseradish Sauce

124

Lasagna

1   cup chopped onion
3   cloves garlic, minced
1   tablespoon CRISCO® Savory Seasonings Roasted Garlic Flavor oil
1   pound extra lean ground beef
2   cans (14½ ounces each) no-salt-added stewed tomatoes
1   can (6 ounces) no-salt-added tomato paste
2   teaspoons dried basil leaves, crushed
1   teaspoon dried oregano leaves, crushed
½   teaspoon sugar
¼   teaspoon black pepper
2   cups low-fat cottage cheese
½   cup grated Parmesan cheese, divided
¼   cup chopped fresh parsley
8   ounces wide lasagna noodles
1   cup (4 ounces) shredded low-moisture part-skim mozzarella
    cheese, divided

Cook and stir onion and garlic in oil in large skillet over medium heat until soft. Push to side of skillet. Add ground beef. Cook, stirring well to crumble beef. Drain, if necessary. Add tomatoes with juice, breaking up tomatoes. Add tomato paste, basil, oregano, sugar and pepper. Stir until well blended. Simmer 30 minutes. Combine cottage cheese, ¼ cup Parmesan cheese and parsley.

Cook noodles 7 minutes in unsalted boiling water. Drain well. Heat oven to 350°F. Place thin layer of meat sauce in 13×9×2-inch pan. Add, in layers, half the noodles, half the cottage cheese mixture, 2 tablespoons Parmesan, ⅓ cup mozzarella and thin layer of sauce. Repeat noodle and cheese layers. Top with remaining sauce and ⅓ cup mozzarella. Bake at 350°F for 45 minutes. Let stand 15 minutes. Cut into 12 rectangles.   *Makes 12 servings*

NUTRIENTS PER SERVING			
Calories	270	Fat	10 g
Cholesterol	55 mg	Sodium	300 mg

Chili con Carne

1 tablespoon CRISCO® Oil
1 cup chopped onion
1 cup chopped green bell pepper
1 pound ground beef round
1 can (28 ounces) whole tomatoes, undrained and chopped
1 can (8 ounces) tomato sauce
1 tablespoon chili powder
1 teaspoon salt
¼ teaspoon black pepper
   Dash of hot pepper sauce (optional)
1 can (30 ounces) kidney beans, undrained

1. Heat oil in large saucepan or Dutch oven on medium heat. Add onion and green pepper. Cook and stir until tender. Add meat. Cook until browned, stirring occasionally. Stir in tomatoes, tomato sauce, chili powder, salt, black pepper and hot pepper sauce (if used). Bring to a boil. Reduce heat to low. Simmer 45 minutes, stirring occasionally.

2. Add beans. Heat thoroughly, stirring occasionally.   *Makes 8 servings*

NUTRIENTS PER SERVING			
Calories	185	Fat	5 g
Cholesterol	35 mg	Sodium	505 mg

127

Mediterranean Meatballs and Couscous

1 can (about 14 ounces) fat-free reduced-sodium chicken broth
2½ cups water
1½ cups couscous
¾ cup golden raisins
¼ cup chopped parsley
3 tablespoons lemon juice, divided
3 teaspoons grated lemon peel, divided
2 teaspoons ground cinnamon, divided
1 teaspoon turmeric
½ teaspoon ground cumin
1 pound ground round beef
½ cup crushed saltine crackers
¼ cup evaporated skimmed milk
½ teaspoon dried oregano leaves

1. Pour chicken broth and water into 2-quart saucepan. Bring to a boil over high heat. Remove from heat. Add couscous, raisins, parsley, 2 tablespoons lemon juice, 2 teaspoons lemon peel, 1½ teaspoons cinnamon, turmeric and cumin. Cover and let stand 5 minutes.

2. Combine beef, crackers, milk, remaining 1 tablespoon lemon juice, 1 teaspoon lemon peel, ½ teaspoon cinnamon and oregano in large bowl. Mix until well blended. Shape into 24 meatballs. Place in large microwavable baking dish. Cover loosely with waxed paper. Microwave at HIGH 4 minutes or until meatballs are cooked through. Stir couscous mixture and spoon onto platter. Top with meatballs. Garnish with lemon and fresh oregano, if desired.

Makes 6 servings

NUTRIENTS PER SERVING			
Calories	434	Fat	11 g
Cholesterol	50 mg	Sodium	180 mg

Mediterranean Meatballs and Couscous

Beef Burgers with Corn Salsa

½ cup frozen corn
½ cup peeled, seeded and chopped tomato
1 can (4 ounces) diced green chilies, divided
1 tablespoon chopped fresh cilantro *or* 1 teaspoon dried
   cilantro leaves
1 tablespoon vinegar
1 teaspoon olive oil
¼ cup fine dry bread crumbs
3 tablespoons skim milk
¼ teaspoon garlic powder
12 ounces 95% lean ground beef

Prepare corn according to package directions, omitting salt; drain. Combine corn, tomato, 2 tablespoons green chilies, cilantro, vinegar and oil in small bowl. Cover and refrigerate.

Preheat broiler. Combine bread crumbs, remaining green chilies, skim milk and garlic powder in medium bowl. Add beef; blend well to combine. Shape to form four ¾-inch-thick patties. Place on broiler pan. Broil 4 inches from heat 6 minutes. Turn and broil 6 to 8 minutes or until beef is no longer pink in center. Spoon salsa over patties. *Makes 4 servings*

NUTRIENTS PER SERVING			
Calories	180	Fat	6 g
Cholesterol	33 mg	Sodium	101 mg

Beef Burgers with Corn Salsa

Apple-icious Lamb Kabobs

1 cup apple juice or cider
2 tablespoons Worcestershire sauce
½ teaspoon lemon pepper
2 cloves garlic, peeled and sliced
1½ pounds fresh American lamb (leg or shoulder), cut into
     1¼-inch cubes
    Apple Barbecue Sauce (page 134)
1 large apple, cut into 12 wedges
    Assorted vegetables, such as green or red bell pepper, onion
     or summer squash, cut into wedges

Combine apple juice, Worcestershire sauce, lemon pepper and garlic in large resealable plastic food storage bag or nonmetal container. Add lamb cubes and coat well. To marinate, refrigerate 2 to 24 hours.

Prepare Apple Barbecue Sauce. Preheat grill or broiler. Remove meat from marinade and thread onto skewers, alternating meat, apple and vegetables. (If using bamboo skewers, soak in water for 20 to 30 minutes before using to prevent them from burning.)

To grill, place kabobs 4 inches from medium coals. Cook about 10 to 12 minutes, turning occasionally and brushing with Apple Barbecue Sauce. To broil, place kabobs on broiler pan sprayed with nonstick cooking spray. Broil 4 inches from heat about 10 to 12 minutes for medium-rare, turning occasionally and brushing with Apple Barbecue Sauce. *Makes 6 servings*

NUTRIENTS PER SERVING			
(not including sauce)			
Calories	165	Fat	5 g
Cholesterol	57 mg	Sodium	62 mg

continued on page 134

Apple-icious Lamb Kabob

Apple-icious Lamb Kabobs, continued

APPLE BARBECUE SAUCE

½ cup apple juice or cider
½ cup finely chopped onion
1 cup chili sauce
½ cup unsweetened applesauce
2 tablespoons packed brown sugar
1 tablespoon Worcestershire sauce
1 teaspoon dry mustard
5 drops hot pepper sauce

Combine apple juice and onion in small saucepan; simmer 2 minutes. Stir in chili sauce, applesauce, brown sugar, Worcestershire sauce, dry mustard and hot pepper sauce. Simmer 10 minutes, stirring occasionally. Remove from heat.

Makes about 2 cups

NUTRIENTS PER SERVING			
Calories	90	Fat	1 g
Cholesterol	0 mg	Sodium	36 mg

Favorite recipe from American Lamb Council

Spring Lamb Skillet

2   teaspoons olive oil
1   pound boneless lamb, cut into 1-inch cubes
2   cups thinly sliced yellow squash
2   cups (about 8 ounces) sliced fresh mushrooms
2   medium tomatoes, seeded and chopped
½   cup sliced green onions
3   cups cooked brown rice
½   teaspoon dried rosemary
½   teaspoon salt
½   teaspoon cracked black pepper

Heat oil in large skillet over medium heat until hot. Add lamb and cook 3 to
5 minutes or until lamb is browned. Remove from skillet; reserve. Add squash,
mushrooms, tomatoes and onions to skillet; cook 2 to 3 minutes or until
vegetables are tender. Stir in rice, rosemary, salt, pepper and reserved lamb.
Cook until heated through.   *Makes 6 servings*

NUTRIENTS PER SERVING			
Calories	258	Fat	8 g
Cholesterol	50 mg	Sodium	313 mg

Favorite recipe from **USA Rice Council**

Pronto Pizza

6 ounces lean fresh ground American lamb
½ teaspoon onion salt
½ teaspoon fennel seeds
¼ teaspoon dried oregano leaves
¼ teaspoon dried basil leaves
⅛ teaspoon red pepper flakes
½ cup chopped bell pepper
½ cup chopped Italian plum tomatoes
1 (10- to 12-inch) prebaked pizza shell
½ cup pizza sauce
1 tablespoon grated Parmesan cheese
¼ cup thinly sliced fresh basil leaves (optional)
½ cup (2 ounces) shredded part-skim mozzarella cheese

Preheat oven to 450°F. Combine lamb, onion salt, fennel seeds, oregano, dried basil and red pepper flakes in small bowl; knead until well blended. Spray nonstick skillet with nonstick cooking spray. Cook and stir lamb over medium-high heat until lightly browned, stirring to separate lamb. Drain on paper towel. In same skillet, cook and stir bell pepper 3 to 4 minutes, stirring occasionally. Add tomatoes; cook and stir 1 minute. Place pizza shell on cookie sheet or pizza pan; top with pizza sauce and vegetables. Sprinkle with Parmesan cheese, fresh basil, cooked lamb and mozzarella cheese. Bake 8 to 10 minutes. Cool 5 minutes and slice into wedges. *Makes 6 to 8 servings*

Microwave Directions: Cook lamb mixture in 2-quart microwavable dish on HIGH (100% power) 3 minutes, stirring several times to crumble lamb. Add bell pepper and tomatoes; microwave on HIGH 2 minutes, stirring once. Drain well. Assemble pizza as directed above.

NUTRIENTS PER SERVING			
Calories	218	Fat	5 g
Cholesterol	20 mg	Sodium	360 mg

Favorite recipe from **American Lamb Council**

Pronto Pizza

Veal in Gingered Sweet Bell Pepper Sauce

 1 teaspoon olive oil
¾ pound veal cutlets, thinly sliced
½ cup skim milk
 1 tablespoon finely chopped fresh tarragon
 2 teaspoons crushed capers
 1 jar (7 ounces) roasted red peppers, drained
 1 tablespoon lemon juice
½ teaspoon freshly grated ginger
½ teaspoon ground black pepper

1. Heat oil in medium saucepan over high heat. Add veal; lightly brown both sides. Reduce heat to medium. Add milk, chopped tarragon and capers. Cook, uncovered, 5 minutes or until veal is fork-tender and milk evaporates.

2. Place roasted peppers, lemon juice, ginger and black pepper in food processor or blender; process until smooth. Set aside.

3. Remove veal from pan with slotted spoon; place in serving dish. Spoon roasted pepper sauce over veal. Sprinkle with cooked capers and fresh tarragon, if desired.   *Makes 4 servings*

NUTRIENTS PER SERVING			
Calories	120	Fat	4 g
Cholesterol	54 mg	Sodium	89 mg

Veal in Gingered Sweet Bell Pepper Sauce

Poultry

● ● ● ● ● ● ● ● ● ●

Crunchy Apple Salsa with Grilled Chicken

2 cups Washington Gala apples, halved, cored and chopped
¾ cup (1 large) Anaheim chili pepper, seeded and chopped
½ cup chopped onion
¼ cup lime juice
Salt and pepper to taste
Grilled Chicken (recipe follows)

Combine all ingredients except chicken and mix well; set aside to allow flavors to blend about 45 minutes. Prepare Grilled Chicken. Serve salsa over or alongside Grilled Chicken. *Makes 3 cups salsa*

Grilled Chicken: Marinate 2 whole boneless, skinless chicken breasts in mixture of ¼ cup dry white wine, ¼ cup apple juice, ½ teaspoon grated lime peel, ½ teaspoon salt and dash pepper for 20 to 30 minutes. Drain and grill over medium-hot coals, turning once, until chicken is no longer pink in center. Makes 4 servings.

NUTRIENTS PER SERVING			
Calories	211	Fat	3 g
Cholesterol	73 mg	Sodium	155 mg

Favorite recipe from **Washington Apple Commission**

Crunchy Apple Salsa with Grilled Chicken

Spicy Marinated Chicken Kababs over Rice

½ cup white wine
¼ cup lime juice
¼ cup vegetable oil
2 cloves garlic, minced
1 jalapeño pepper, seeded and finely chopped
2 tablespoons chopped fresh cilantro
½ teaspoon salt
½ teaspoon ground black pepper
1½ pounds boneless, skinless chicken breast, cut into 1-inch
      cubes
1 medium-size red onion, cut into 1-inch pieces
2 medium-size red or green bell peppers, cut into 1-inch pieces
2 medium-size yellow squash, cut into 1-inch pieces
12 wooden or metal skewers*
      Vegetable cooking spray
3 cups hot cooked rice

Combine wine, lime juice, oil, garlic, jalapeño, cilantro, salt and black pepper in gallon size resealable plastic food storage bag. Add chicken, onion, bell peppers and squash. Seal; turn to coat. Marinate in refrigerator 30 to 45 minutes. Remove chicken and vegetables. Place marinade in small saucepan. Bring to a boil over medium-high heat; keep warm. Alternate chicken and vegetables on skewers. Place on broiler rack coated with cooking spray; brush with marinade. Broil 4 to 6 inches from heat 8 to 10 minutes, turning and basting frequently with marinade. Serve over hot rice. *Makes 6 servings*

*Soak wooden skewers in water before using to prevent burning.

NUTRIENTS PER SERVING			
Calories	280	Fat	5 g
Cholesterol	73 mg	Sodium	262 mg

Favorite recipe from **USA Rice Council**

Spicy Marinated Chicken Kababs over Rice

Spinach-Stuffed Chicken Breasts

2   boneless skinless chicken breasts (8 ounces each), halved
5   ounces frozen chopped spinach, thawed, well drained
2   tablespoons freshly grated Parmesan cheese
1   teaspoon grated lemon peel
¼   teaspoon ground black pepper
    Olive oil-flavored nonstick cooking spray
1   cup thinly sliced mushrooms
6   slices (2 ounces) thinly sliced low-fat turkey-ham
1   cup white grape juice

1. Trim fat from chicken; discard. Place each chicken breast between 2 sheets of plastic wrap. Pound with meat mallet until chicken is about ¼ inch thick.

2. Preheat oven to 350°F. Pat spinach dry with paper towels. Combine spinach, Parmesan, lemon peel and black pepper in large bowl. Spray small nonstick skillet with cooking spray; add mushrooms. Cook and stir over medium heat 3 to 4 minutes or until tender.

3. Arrange 1½ slices turkey-ham over each chicken breast. Spread each with one-fourth of spinach mixture. Top each with mushrooms. Beginning with longer side, roll chicken tightly. Tie with kitchen string.

4. Place stuffed chicken breasts in 9-inch square baking pan, seam side down. Lightly spray chicken with cooking spray. Pour white grape juice over top. Bake 30 minutes or until chicken is no longer pink.

5. Remove string; cut chicken rolls into ½-inch diagonal slices. Arrange on plate. Pour pan juices over chicken. Garnish as desired.   *Makes 4 servings*

NUTRIENTS PER SERVING			
Calories	187	Fat	4 g
Cholesterol	71 mg	Sodium	302 mg

Spinach-Stuffed Chicken Breasts

Chicken with Zucchini and Tomatoes

8 broiler-fryer chicken thighs, boned, skinned
1 tablespoon olive oil
2 small zucchini, cut in ¼-inch slices
1 can (14½ ounces) stewed tomatoes
½ teaspoon Italian seasoning
¼ teaspoon salt
⅛ teaspoon pepper

In large skillet, heat oil over medium-high heat. Add chicken and cook, turning, 10 minutes or until browned. Drain off excess fat. Add zucchini, tomatoes, Italian seasoning, salt and pepper. Reduce heat to medium-low; cover and cook about 10 minutes more or until chicken and zucchini are fork-tender.

Makes 4 servings

NUTRIENTS PER SERVING			
Calories	232	Fat	9 g
Cholesterol	114 mg	Sodium	373 mg

Favorite recipe from Delmarva Poultry Industry, Inc.

Broiled Lemon Chicken

4 skinless boneless chicken breast halves (about 1 pound)
¼ cup HEINZ® Worcestershire Sauce
2 tablespoons lemon juice
1 teaspoon minced garlic
½ teaspoon pepper
½ teaspoon grated lemon peel
   Vegetable oil

Lightly flatten chicken breasts to uniform thickness; place in shallow pan or bowl. For marinade, combine Worcestershire sauce and next 4 ingredients; pour over chicken. Cover; marinate 30 minutes, turning once. Place chicken on broiler pan; brush lightly with oil. Broil, 4 to 5 inches from heat source, 3 to 4 minutes; turn. Brush with marinade, then with oil; broil an additional 3 to 4 minutes.   *Makes 4 servings*

NUTRIENTS PER SERVING			
Calories	142	Fat	3 g
Cholesterol	66 mg	Sodium	239 mg

Lemon-Dilly Chicken Sauté

4 broiler-fryer chicken breast halves, boned, skinned
½ cup dry bread crumbs
1 teaspoon lemon pepper
¼ teaspoon dried dill weed
3 tablespoons lemon juice
2 tablespoons olive oil

With meat mallet or similar flattening utensil, pound chicken breasts to ¼-inch thickness. In shallow dish, mix together bread crumbs, lemon pepper and dill. In second dish, place lemon juice. Add chicken, one piece at a time, first to lemon juice, then to crumb mixture, turning to coat all sides. In large nonstick skillet, heat oil over medium-high heat. Add chicken and cook, turning, about 10 minutes or until chicken is brown and fork-tender.   *Makes 4 servings*

NUTRIENTS PER SERVING			
Calories	243	Fat	9 g
Cholesterol	68 mg	Sodium	187 mg

Favorite recipe from **Delmarva Poultry Industry, Inc.**

Chicken & Tortilla Casserole

¼ cup low sodium chicken broth, defatted and divided
½ cup finely chopped red bell pepper
½ cup finely chopped green bell pepper
½ cup finely chopped red onion
1 can (28 ounces) low sodium tomatoes, undrained
¼ cup GUILTLESS GOURMET® Spicy Nacho Dip
3 ounces (about 60) GUILTLESS GOURMET® Unsalted Baked
    Tortilla Chips, divided
1 cup cooked and shredded boneless chicken breast
    Fresh herb sprig (optional)

NACHO SAUCE
¾ cup GUILTLESS GOURMET® Spicy Nacho Dip
¼ cup low fat sour cream
¼ cup skim milk

Preheat oven to 350°F. Heat 2 tablespoons broth in medium nonstick skillet until hot. Add peppers and onion; cook about 5 minutes, stirring often. Add remaining 2 tablespoons broth and cook until peppers are soft. Remove from heat; set aside. Drain off about ¾ juice from tomatoes; discard. Coarsely chop tomatoes. To assemble casserole, spread ¼ cup nacho dip on bottom of 1½- to 2-quart casserole dish. Top with layer of tortilla chips (about 30). Cover with pepper mixture, followed by another layer of tortilla chips (about 30). Evenly spread chicken over chips; top with tomatoes and remaining juice. Combine Nacho Sauce ingredients in small saucepan; heat over medium heat 2 to 3 minutes or until warm. Drizzle half the mixture evenly over tomato layer.

Cover and bake 25 to 35 minutes or until mixture bubbles. Drizzle with remaining nacho sauce. Garnish, if desired. *Makes 4 servings*

NUTRIENTS PER SERVING			
Calories	247	Fat	3 g
Cholesterol	22 mg	Sodium	400 mg

Chicken & Tortilla Casserole

Maui Chicken Sandwich

1 can (8 ounces) DOLE® Pineapple Slices
½ teaspoon dried oregano leaves, crushed
¼ teaspoon garlic powder
4 skinless, boneless small chicken breast halves
½ cup light prepared Thousand Island salad dressing
½ cup finely chopped jicama or water chestnuts
¼ teaspoon ground red pepper (optional)
4 whole grain or whole wheat sandwich rolls
   DOLE® Red or Green Bell Pepper, sliced into rings or
      shredded DOLE® Iceberg Lettuce

• **Combine** undrained pineapple, oregano and garlic powder in shallow, non-metallic dish. Add chicken; turn to coat all sides. Cover and marinate 15 minutes in refrigerator.

• **Grill** or broil chicken and pineapple, brushing occasionally with marinade, 5 to 8 minutes on each side or until chicken is no longer pink in center and pineapple is golden brown. Discard any remaining marinade.

• **Combine** dressing, jicama and red pepper. Spread on rolls. Top with chicken, pineapple and bell pepper rings. Serve open-face, if desired.

Makes 4 servings

Prep time: 10 minutes
Marinate time: 15 minutes
Cook time: 15 minutes

NUTRIENTS PER SERVING			
Calories	284	Fat	8 g
Cholesterol	82 mg	Sodium	452 mg

Maui Chicken Sandwich

Rosemary Chicken with Asparagus Lemon Rice

¼ cup dry white wine
3 cloves garlic, minced
1 tablespoon finely chopped fresh rosemary
1 tablespoon vegetable oil
1 tablespoon reduced-sodium soy sauce
1 teaspoon sugar
½ teaspoon ground black pepper
6 boneless, skinless chicken breast halves (about 2¼ pounds)
  Vegetable cooking spray
3 cups cooked rice (cooked in low-sodium chicken broth)
10 spears asparagus, blanched and cut into 1-inch pieces
    (¼ pound)
1 teaspoon grated lemon peel
1 teaspoon lemon pepper
½ teaspoon salt
  Lemon slices for garnish
  Fresh rosemary sprigs for garnish

Combine wine, garlic, rosemary, oil, soy sauce, sugar and pepper in large shallow glass dish. Add chicken, turning to coat; cover and marinate in refrigerator at least 1 hour. Heat large skillet coated with cooking spray over medium-high heat until hot. Add chicken and marinade; cook 7 minutes on each side or until brown and no longer pink in center. Combine rice, asparagus, lemon peel, lemon pepper and salt in large bowl. To serve, spoon rice on individual serving plates. Cut chicken into strips; fan over rice. Garnish with lemon and rosemary.

Makes 6 servings

NUTRIENTS PER SERVING			
Calories	294	Fat	6 g
Cholesterol	73 mg	Sodium	437 mg

Favorite recipe from **USA Rice Council**

Rosemary Chicken with Asparagus Lemon Rice

Balsamic Chicken

6   boneless skinless chicken breast halves
1½   teaspoons fresh rosemary, minced *or* ½ teaspoon dried
       rosemary
2   cloves garlic, minced
¾   teaspoon pepper
½   teaspoon salt
1   tablespoon olive oil
¼   cup good-quality balsamic vinegar

1. Rinse chicken and pat dry. Combine rosemary, garlic, pepper and salt in small bowl; mix well. Place chicken in large bowl; drizzle chicken with oil and rub with spice mixture. Cover and refrigerate overnight.

2. Preheat oven to 450°F. Spray heavy roasting pan or iron skillet with nonstick cooking spray. Place chicken in pan; bake 10 minutes. Turn chicken over, stirring in 3 to 4 tablespoons water if drippings are beginning to stick to pan.

3. Bake about 10 minutes or until chicken is golden brown and no longer pink in center. If pan is dry, stir in another 1 to 2 tablespoons water to loosen drippings.

4. Drizzle balsamic vinegar over chicken in pan. Transfer chicken to plates. Stir liquid in pan; drizzle over chicken. Garnish, if desired.   *Makes 6 servings*

NUTRIENTS PER SERVING			
Calories	174	Fat	5 g
Cholesterol	73 mg	Sodium	242 mg

Chicken with Mandarin Orange and Water Chestnut Sauce

1 can (11 ounces) mandarin oranges, drained
1 can (8 ounces) sliced water chestnuts, drained
4 teaspoons packed brown sugar
2 tablespoons white vinegar
1 tablespoon reduced-sodium soy sauce
2 teaspoons cornstarch
¼ cup water
1½ cups chicken broth or stock
4 split chicken breast halves, skinned and boned

In small saucepan, combine mandarin oranges, water chestnuts, brown sugar, vinegar, soy sauce and cornstarch dissolved in ¼ cup water. Cook until mixture becomes clear and thickens, about 4 to 5 minutes, stirring occasionally. Remove from heat. In large skillet, bring broth to a simmer. Pound chicken breasts with meat mallet to ½-inch thickness. Place chicken in skillet; cover and simmer over medium-low heat about 8 to 10 minutes or until chicken is no longer pink in center. Remove chicken from poaching liquid. Place on serving platter. Heat sauce if needed; spoon sauce over chicken.

Makes 4 servings

NUTRIENTS PER SERVING			
Calories	253	Fat	5 g
Cholesterol	73 mg	Sodium	755 mg

Skillet Chicken Pot Pie

1   can (10¾ ounces) fat-free reduced-sodium cream of chicken
     soup
1¼ cups skim milk, divided
1   package (10 ounces) frozen mixed vegetables
2   cups diced cooked chicken
½ teaspoon ground black pepper
1   cup buttermilk biscuit baking mix
¼ teaspoon summer savory or parsley

1. Heat soup, 1 cup milk, vegetables, chicken and pepper in medium skillet over medium heat until mixture comes to a boil.

2. Combine biscuit mix and summer savory in small bowl. Stir in 3 to 4 tablespoons milk just until soft batter is formed. Drop batter by tablespoonfuls onto chicken mixture to make 6 dumplings. Partially cover and simmer 12 minutes or until dumplings are cooked through, spooning liquid from pot pie over dumplings once or twice during cooking. Garnish with additional summer savory, if desired. *Makes 6 servings*

NUTRIENTS PER SERVING			
Calories	241	Fat	5 g
Cholesterol	33 mg	Sodium	422 mg

Skillet Chicken Pot Pie

Tomato Chutney Chicken

4   broiler-fryer chicken breast halves, boned, skinned
1   can (16 ounces) tomatoes with juice, cut up
1   cup peeled and chopped cooking apple
¼   cup chopped onion
¼   cup chopped green bell pepper
¼   cup golden raisins
2   tablespoons brown sugar
2   tablespoons lemon juice
1   teaspoon grated lemon peel
1   clove garlic, minced
¼   teaspoon red pepper flakes
½   teaspoon ground cinnamon
¼   teaspoon salt

158

In large skillet, place tomatoes, apple, onion, green bell pepper, raisins, brown sugar, lemon juice, lemon peel, garlic, red pepper flakes and cinnamon; stir to mix. Cook, stirring, over medium-high heat until mixture boils. Sprinkle salt over chicken breasts. Place chicken over tomato mixture. Reduce heat to medium-low; cover and cook, stirring and turning frequently, about 15 minutes or until chicken is fork-tender. Arrange chicken on serving platter; spoon sauce over chicken.

Makes 4 servings

NUTRIENTS PER SERVING			
Calories	230	Fat	4 g
Cholesterol	68 mg	Sodium	364 mg

Favorite recipe from **Delmarva Poultry Industry, Inc.**

Tomato Chutney Chicken

Chicken Chop Suey

1 package (1 ounce) dried black Chinese mushrooms
3 tablespoons reduced-sodium soy sauce
1 tablespoon cornstarch
1 pound boneless skinless chicken breasts or thighs
2 cloves garlic, minced
1 tablespoon peanut or vegetable oil
½ cup thinly sliced celery
½ cup sliced water chestnuts
½ cup bamboo shoots
1 cup chicken broth
   Hot cooked white rice or chow mein noodles
   Thinly sliced green onions (optional)

Place mushrooms in small bowl; cover with warm water. Soak 20 minutes to soften. Drain; squeeze out excess water. Discard stems; quarter caps.

Blend soy sauce with cornstarch in cup until smooth.

Cut chicken into 1-inch pieces; toss with garlic in small bowl. Heat wok or large skillet over medium-high heat; add oil. Add chicken mixture and celery; stir-fry 2 minutes. Add water chestnuts and bamboo shoots; stir-fry 1 minute. Add broth and mushrooms; cook and stir 3 minutes or until chicken is no longer pink.

Stir soy sauce mixture and add to wok. Cook and stir 1 to 2 minutes until sauce boils and thickens. Serve over rice. Garnish with green onions, if desired.

Makes 4 servings

NUTRIENTS PER SERVING			
Calories	208	Fat	6 g
Cholesterol	58 mg	Sodium	657 mg

Chicken Chop Suey

Grilled Chicken Sienna

1 package (about 1¼ pounds) PERDUE® Fit 'n Easy® fresh
     skinless & boneless chicken breasts & thighs
2 tablespoons lemon juice
1 tablespoon olive oil
1 teaspoon dried Italian herb seasoning
    Salt and ground pepper to taste
    Pinch sugar
1 cup seeded and finely diced tomato
3 cups arugula leaves, well washed

Trim off and discard visible fat from chicken. In shallow baking dish, combine lemon juice, olive oil and Italian seasoning. Add chicken; cover and marinate in refrigerator 1 to 2 hours. Add pinch of salt, pepper and sugar to tomato; set aside.

Prepare outdoor grill or preheat broiler. Drain chicken, reserving marinade. Grill or broil chicken 6 to 8 inches from heat source 15 to 25 minutes until cooked through. Meanwhile, in small saucepan, bring marinade to a boil. Turn chicken 2 to 3 times during cooking and brush with boiled marinade. Slice chicken and arrange on bed of arugula; top with tomato mixture.

Makes 6 servings

NUTRIENTS PER SERVING			
Calories	139	Fat	5 g
Cholesterol	67 mg	Sodium	85 mg

Grilled Chicken Sienna

Busy Day Oven-Fried Chicken Breasts

¾ cup plain dry bread crumbs
¼ cup all-purpose flour
1 teaspoon paprika
1 teaspoon poultry seasoning
1 teaspoon onion salt
½ teaspoon garlic powder
½ teaspoon dried thyme leaves
¼ teaspoon pepper
1 tablespoon plus 1½ teaspoons CRISCO® Oil
4 whole chicken breasts, skinned and split (about 4 pounds)

1. Heat oven to 400°F.

2. Combine bread crumbs, flour, paprika, poultry seasoning, onion salt, garlic powder, thyme and pepper in shallow dish. Stir with fork until well blended. Add oil gradually. Toss with fork to blend.

3. Moisten chicken with water. Roll in coating mixture. Place in single layer in 15½×10½×¾-inch jelly roll pan or other large shallow pan. Sprinkle any remaining crumb mixture over chicken.

4. Bake at 400°F for 30 minutes or until chicken is no longer pink in center.

Makes 8 servings

NUTRIENTS PER SERVING			
Calories	200	Fat	5 g
Cholesterol	65 mg	Sodium	145 mg

Carefree Golden Oven Stew

4   small chicken breast halves, skinned
1   lemon, halved
½   teaspoon salt
⅟₁₆ teaspoon pepper
1   Golden Delicious apple, sliced
1   small onion, sliced lengthwise
1   cup mushrooms, halved
½   cup sliced carrots
⅔   cup chicken broth
¼   cup white wine
1   teaspoon dried tarragon leaves, crushed
1   teaspoon fresh chopped parsley

Rub chicken with lemon and let stand 15 minutes. Sprinkle with salt and pepper. Place chicken breasts in 2-quart baking dish. Add apple, onion, mushrooms and carrots. In separate bowl combine chicken broth, wine and tarragon; pour over chicken mixture. Sprinkle with parsley. Bake, covered, at 350°F about 1 hour or until chicken is tender.   *Makes 4 servings*

NUTRIENTS PER SERVING			
Calories	255	Fat	8 g
Cholesterol	83 mg	Sodium	517 mg

Favorite recipe from **Washington Apple Commission**

Chicken Florentine with Lemon Mustard Sauce

2 whole boneless skinless chicken breasts, halved (1 pound)
¼ cup EGG BEATERS® Healthy Real Egg Product
½ cup plain dry bread crumbs
1 teaspoon dried basil leaves
1 teaspoon garlic powder
2 tablespoons FLEISCHMANN'S® Sweet Unsalted Margarine,
    divided
⅓ cup water
2 tablespoons GREY POUPON® Dijon Mustard
2 tablespoons lemon juice
1 tablespoon sugar
1 (10-ounce) package frozen chopped spinach, cooked, well
    drained and kept warm

Pound chicken breasts to ¼-inch thickness. Pour Egg Beaters® into shallow bowl. Combine bread crumbs, basil and garlic. Dip chicken breasts into Egg Beaters®, then coat with bread crumb mixture.

In large nonstick skillet, over medium-high heat, melt 1 tablespoon margarine. Add chicken; cook for 5 to 7 minutes on each side or until browned and no longer pink in center. Remove chicken from skillet; keep warm. In same skillet, melt remaining margarine; stir in water, mustard, lemon juice and sugar. Simmer 1 minute or until thickened. To serve, arrange chicken on serving platter. Top with spinach; drizzle with lemon-mustard sauce. Garnish as desired. *Makes 4 servings*

Prep time: 25 minutes
Cook time: 15 minutes

NUTRIENTS PER SERVING			
Calories	278	Fat	8 g
Cholesterol	69 mg	Sodium	468 mg

Chicken Florentine with Lemon Mustard Sauce

SMUCKER'S® Orange Chili Barbecue Sauce

1 cup SMUCKER'S® Sweet Orange Marmalade
1 cup tomato sauce or crushed tomatoes packed in
    tomato purée
2 tablespoons red wine vinegar
2 tablespoons chili powder
1 teaspoon ground cumin
1 teaspoon chopped garlic
½ teaspoon salt
¼ teaspoon ground red pepper or hot pepper sauce (for a
    spicier sauce)

Combine all ingredients in a small saucepan and mix well. Heat the sauce until it comes to a boil, stirring constantly. Simmer for 1 minute.

Use the sauce immediately as a marinade and baste for grilled chicken, ribs, beef or pork. Or, cool and store in the refrigerator for future use.

Makes 6 servings

Microwave Directions: Combine all ingredients in a microwave-safe bowl. Cover with plastic wrap and heat on HIGH (100% power) for 2 minutes. Stir; cover and heat for 1 minute.

Prep time: 5 minutes
Cook time: 1 to 2 minutes

NUTRIENTS PER SERVING			
Calories	160	Fat	1 g
Cholesterol	0 mg	Sodium	459 mg

Honey-Orange Chicken Legs

4 whole broiler-fryer chicken legs (thigh and drumstick
  attached), skinned, fat trimmed
½ teaspoon salt
¼ teaspoon pepper
6 tablespoons orange juice
4 teaspoons honey
1½ teaspoons Worcestershire sauce
½ teaspoon dry mustard

In baking pan, place chicken in single layer. Sprinkle salt and pepper over chicken. Bake in 350°F oven 25 minutes. In small dish, mix together orange juice, honey, Worcestershire sauce and mustard. Spoon sauce over chicken. Bake, basting frequently, 30 minutes more or until chicken is brown and fork-tender. *Makes 4 servings*

NUTRIENTS PER SERVING			
Calories	193	Fat	5 g
Cholesterol	104 mg	Sodium	398 mg

Favorite recipe from Delmarva Poultry Industry, Inc.

Oven Chicken & Rice

1 package (4.3 ounces) RICE-A-RONI® Long Grain & Wild Rice
  Pilaf
4 bone-in chicken breast halves
½ teaspoon dried thyme leaves or dried basil leaves
¼ teaspoon garlic powder
1 tablespoon margarine or butter, melted
½ teaspoon paprika
1 cup chopped tomato or red bell pepper

170

1. Heat oven to 375°F. In 11×7-inch glass baking dish or 1½-quart casserole, combine 1¼ cups water, rice and contents of seasoning packet; mix well.

2. Place chicken over rice. Sprinkle evenly with thyme and garlic powder. Brush with margarine; sprinkle with paprika. Cover with foil; bake 45 minutes. Stir in tomato. Bake, uncovered, 15 minutes or until liquid is absorbed and chicken is no longer pink in center.   *Makes 4 servings*

NUTRIENTS PER SERVING			
Calories	280	Fat	5 g
Cholesterol	70 mg	Sodium	1,000 mg

Chicken Breasts with Orange Basil Pesto

½ cup fresh basil leaves
2 tablespoons grated orange peel
2 cloves garlic
3 tablespoons Florida orange juice
1 tablespoon Dijon mustard
2 teaspoons olive oil
6 chicken breast halves

Preheat broiler. Place basil, orange peel and garlic in food processor; process until finely chopped. Add orange juice, mustard, oil, and salt and pepper to taste; process several seconds or until paste forms. Spread equal amounts of basil mixture under skin and on bone side of each chicken breast. Place chicken, skin-side down, on broiler pan; place pan 4 inches from heat source. Broil 10 minutes. Turn chicken over and broil 10 to 12 minutes or until chicken is no longer pink in center. If chicken browns too quickly, cover with foil. Remove skin from chicken before serving.   *Makes 6 servings*

NUTRIENTS PER SERVING			
Calories	206	Fat	6 g
Cholesterol	91 mg	Sodium	113 mg

Favorite recipe from **Florida Department of Citrus**

Mexican Lasagna

½ pound lean ground turkey
½ cup chopped onion
½ cup chopped bell pepper
½ teaspoon black pepper
½ teaspoon dried basil leaves, crushed
 1 can (8 ounces) low sodium tomato sauce
 1 cup GUILTLESS GOURMET® Salsa (mild, medium or hot),
      divided
 1 cup low fat cottage cheese
½ cup GUILTLESS GOURMET® Nacho Dip (mild or spicy)
    Nonstick cooking spray
 1 bag (7 ounces) GUILTLESS GOURMET® Unsalted Baked
      Tortilla Chips, crushed*
    Carrot strip and fresh parsley sprig (optional)

Preheat oven to 350°F. Cook turkey, onion, bell pepper, black pepper and basil in nonstick skillet over medium heat until turkey is no longer pink, breaking up meat and stirring occasionally. Stir in tomato sauce and ½ cup salsa; remove from heat. Combine cottage cheese and nacho dip in small bowl. Coat 8×8-inch baking dish with cooking spray. Set aside.

To assemble lasagna, place ⅓ of crushed chips in bottom of prepared dish, spreading to cover. Top with half the turkey mixture. Spread half the cheese mixture over turkey mixture. Repeat layers once. Top with remaining crushed chips; pour remaining salsa evenly over chips. Bake 30 minutes or until heated through. Let stand 10 minutes before serving. Garnish with carrot and parsley.

Makes 4 servings

*Crush tortilla chips in the original bag or crush between two pieces of waxed paper with a rolling pin.

NUTRIENTS PER SERVING			
Calories	257	Fat	2 g
Cholesterol	20 mg	Sodium	495 mg

Turkey Gyros

1 turkey tenderloin (8 ounces)
1½ teaspoons Greek seasoning
1 cucumber
⅔ cup plain nonfat yogurt
¼ cup finely chopped onion
2 teaspoons dried dill weed
2 teaspoons fresh lemon juice
1 teaspoon olive oil
4 pita breads
1½ cups washed and shredded romaine lettuce
1 tomato, thinly sliced
2 tablespoons crumbled feta cheese

1. Cut turkey tenderloin across the grain into ¼-inch slices. Place turkey slices on plate; lightly sprinkle both sides with Greek seasoning. Let stand 5 minutes.

2. Cut two-thirds of cucumber into thin slices. Finely chop remaining cucumber. Combine chopped cucumber, yogurt, onion, dill weed and lemon juice in small bowl.

3. Heat olive oil in large skillet over medium heat until hot. Add turkey. Cook 2 minutes on each side or until cooked through. Wrap 2 pita breads in paper toweling. Microwave at HIGH (100% power) 30 seconds or just until warmed. Repeat with remaining pita breads. Divide lettuce, tomato, cucumber slices, turkey, cheese and yogurt-cucumber sauce evenly among pita breads. Fold edges over and secure with wooden picks. *Makes 4 servings*

NUTRIENTS PER SERVING			
Calories	319	Fat	4 g
Cholesterol	55 mg	Sodium	477 mg

Turkey Gyro

Barbecue Bacon Meatloaf

 2 packages (1 pound each) LOUIS RICH® Ground Turkey
12 slices LOUIS RICH® Turkey Bacon, diced
 1 cup quick-cooking oats, uncooked
 1 medium onion, finely chopped
½ cup barbecue sauce
 2 large egg whites
 1 tablespoon Worcestershire sauce

Mix all ingredients in large bowl. Press mixture into ungreased 9×5-inch loaf pan. Top with additional barbecue sauce, if desired. Bake at 375°F for 1 hour 15 minutes. Allow to stand 10 minutes before slicing.   *Makes 10 servings*

Note: Meatloaf ingredients may be combined 1 day ahead and refrigerated. Bake at 375°F for 1½ hours.

NUTRIENTS PER SERVING			
Calories	215	Fat	9 g
Cholesterol	70 mg	Sodium	525 mg

Spiced Turkey, Squash and Apple Medley

1½ pounds Turkey Thighs, skin removed
 1 pound acorn squash, cut crosswise into 1-inch rings
 1 pound cooking apples, cored and cut crosswise into ½-inch rings
¼ cup apple juice
 3 tablespoons packed brown sugar
½ teaspoon ground cinnamon
¼ teaspoon ground nutmeg

1. Place turkey thighs to one side of 13×9×2-inch baking dish. Alternately layer squash and apple rings in other side of dish.

2. Combine apple juice, brown sugar and spices; pour over turkey, squash and apples. Cover with foil and bake 1 hour in 350°F oven; uncover and baste with juices. Bake, uncovered, 15 minutes or until internal temperature of thighs registers 180°F on meat thermometer.   *Makes 4 servings*

NUTRIENTS PER SERVING			
Calories	283	Fat	5 g
Cholesterol	85 mg	Sodium	97 mg

Favorite recipe from **National Turkey Federation**

Barbecued Turkey Tenderloins

1½ cups (12-ounce can) lemon-lime soda
¼ cup soy sauce
¼ cup vegetable oil
1 teaspoon horseradish powder
1 teaspoon garlic powder
1 pound Turkey Tenderloins, cut in half lengthwise
  Nonstick cooking spray

1. Combine soda, soy sauce, oil, horseradish powder and garlic powder in resealable plastic freezer bag. Add turkey tenderloins; seal bag and turn to coat. Refrigerate at least 2 hours. Remove grill rack from charcoal grill and lightly coat with cooking spray; set aside. Preheat grill for direct-heat cooking.

2. Position grill rack over hot coals. Remove turkey from bag and discard marinade. Place turkey tenderloins on grill rack and cook 5 to 6 minutes per side or until turkey is no longer pink in center.   *Makes 4 servings*

NUTRIENTS PER SERVING			
Calories	157	Fat	4 g
Cholesterol	70 mg	Sodium	242 mg

Favorite recipe from **National Turkey Federation**

Fusilli Pizzaiola with Turkey Meatballs

1   pound ground turkey breast
1   egg, lightly beaten
1   tablespoon skim milk
¼   cup Italian-seasoned dry bread crumbs
2   tablespoons chopped fresh parsley
¼   teaspoon ground black pepper, divided
½   cup *each* chopped onion and grated carrots
1   clove garlic, minced
2   teaspoons olive oil
2   cans (14½ ounces each) no-salt-added tomatoes, undrained
2   tablespoons chopped fresh basil
1   tablespoon no-salt-added tomato paste
½   teaspoon dried thyme leaves
1   bay leaf
8   ounces uncooked fusilli or other spiral-shaped pasta

1. Preheat oven to 350°F. Combine turkey, egg and milk; blend in bread crumbs, parsley and ⅛ teaspoon black pepper. With wet hands, shape mixture into small balls. Spray baking sheet with nonstick cooking spray. Arrange meatballs on baking sheet. Bake 25 minutes or until no longer pink in center.

2. Place onion, carrots, garlic and oil in saucepan. Cook and stir over high heat 5 minutes. Add tomatoes, basil, tomato paste, thyme, bay leaf and remaining ⅛ teaspoon black pepper; bring to a boil. Simmer 25 minutes over low heat; add meatballs. Cover; simmer until sauce thickens slightly. Discard bay leaf.

3. Cook pasta according to package directions, omitting salt. Drain. Place in serving bowl; top with meatballs and sauce.   *Makes 4 servings*

NUTRIENTS PER SERVING			
Calories	330	Fat	10 g
Cholesterol	116 mg	Sodium	111 mg

Fusilli Pizzaiola with Turkey Meatballs

Seafood

● ● ● ● ● ● ● ● ●

Shrimp in Tomatillo Sauce over Rice

1   teaspoon olive oil
¼   cup chopped onion
1   cup GUILTLESS GOURMET® Green Tomatillo Salsa
¾   cup white wine
     Juice of ½ lemon
12   ounces medium-size raw shrimp, peeled and deveined
4   cups hot cooked white rice
     Lemon peel strip (optional)

Heat oil in large nonstick skillet over medium-high heat until hot. Add onion; cook and stir until onion is translucent. Add salsa, wine and juice, stirring just until mixture begins to boil. Reduce heat to medium-low; simmer 10 minutes. Add shrimp; cook about 2 minutes or until shrimp turn pink and opaque, stirring occasionally. To serve, place 1 cup rice in each of 4 individual serving bowls. Pour shrimp mixture evenly over rice. Garnish with lemon peel, if desired.

Makes 4 servings

NUTRIENTS PER SERVING			
Calories	274	Fat	2 g
Cholesterol	130 mg	Sodium	479 mg

Shrimp in Tomatillo Sauce over Rice

Broccoli, Scallop and Linguine Toss

12   ounces fresh or frozen scallops
2   medium onions, cut in half lengthwise and sliced
1   cup apple juice
2   tablespoons dry white wine
2   cloves garlic, minced
2   teaspoons dried marjoram leaves
1   teaspoon dried basil leaves
¼   teaspoon pepper
3   cups broccoli flowerets
¼   cup water
4   teaspoons cornstarch
1½   cups chopped seeded tomatoes
¼   cup grated Parmesan cheese
4   cups cooked linguine

Cut large scallops into 1-inch pieces. Combine onions, apple juice, wine, garlic, marjoram, basil and pepper in large skillet. Bring to a boil over high heat. Add broccoli; return to a boil. Reduce heat to medium-low. Cover and simmer 7 minutes; add scallops. Return to a boil; reduce heat. Cover and simmer 1 to 2 minutes or until scallops are opaque. Remove scallops and vegetables.

Combine water and cornstarch in small bowl. Stir into mixture in skillet. Cook and stir over medium heat until mixture boils and thickens. Cook and stir 2 minutes more. Stir in tomatoes and cheese; heat through. Return scallops and vegetables to skillet; heat through. Toss mixture with linguine.

Makes 4 servings

NUTRIENTS PER SERVING			
Calories	248	Fat	4 g
Cholesterol	33 mg	Sodium	309 mg

Broccoli, Scallop and Linguine Toss

Shrimp Pita

¾ cup olive oil
½ cup red wine vinegar
2 medium onions, chopped, divided
2 cloves garlic, minced, divided
2 teaspoons Italian seasoning, divided
1 pound medium shrimp, peeled and deveined
2 medium red or green bell peppers, julienned
4 cups fresh spinach leaves, stems removed and torn
3 cups cooked brown rice
1 teaspoon salt
½ teaspoon ground black pepper
3 pieces pita bread (about 6 inches), each cut in half

Combine olive oil, vinegar, ½ cup chopped onion, 1 clove garlic and 1 teaspoon Italian seasoning in large bowl. Add shrimp; stir until well coated. Cover and marinate in refrigerator 4 hours or overnight.

Thoroughly drain shrimp; discard marinade. Heat large skillet over medium-high heat until hot. Add shrimp, remaining onion, bell peppers, spinach and remaining 1 clove garlic; sauté 3 to 5 minutes or until shrimp are no longer pink and spinach is wilted. Add rice, remaining 1 teaspoon Italian seasoning, salt and black pepper. Cook and stir 2 to 3 minutes or until flavors are well blended. To serve, fill each pita with ½ to ¾ cup rice mixture.

Makes 6 servings

NUTRIENTS PER SERVING			
Calories	296	Fat	6 g
Cholesterol	61 mg	Sodium	677 mg

Favorite recipe from **USA Rice Council**

Shrimp Pita

Barbecued Shrimp with Spicy Rice

1 pound large shrimp, peeled and deveined
4 wooden* or metal skewers
Vegetable cooking spray
⅓ cup prepared barbecue sauce
Spicy Rice (recipe follows)

Thread shrimp on skewers. To broil in oven, place on broiler rack coated with cooking spray. Broil 4 to 5 inches from heat 4 minutes. Brush with barbecue sauce. Turn and brush with remaining barbecue sauce. Broil 2 to 4 minutes longer or until shrimp are done. To cook on outdoor grill, cook skewered shrimp over hot coals 4 minutes. Brush with barbecue sauce. Turn and brush with remaining barbecue sauce. Grill 4 to 5 minutes longer or until shrimp are done. Serve with Spicy Rice. *Makes 4 servings*

*Soak wooden skewers in water before using to prevent burning.

SPICY RICE

½ cup sliced green onions
½ cup minced carrots
½ cup minced red bell pepper
1 jalapeño or serrano pepper, minced
1 tablespoon vegetable oil
2 cups cooked rice (cooked in chicken broth)
2 tablespoons snipped cilantro
1 tablespoon lime juice
1 teaspoon soy sauce
Hot pepper sauce to taste

Cook onions, carrots, bell pepper and jalapeño pepper in oil in large skillet over medium-high heat until tender crisp. Stir in rice, cilantro, lime juice, soy sauce and pepper sauce; cook until thoroughly heated.

continued on page 188

Barbecued Shrimp with Spicy Rice

Barbecued Shrimp with Spicy Rice, continued

Microwave Directions: Combine onions, carrots, bell pepper, jalapeño pepper and oil in 2-quart microproof baking dish. Cook on HIGH (100% power) 2 to 3 minutes or until vegetables are tender crisp. Add rice, cilantro, lime juice, soy sauce and pepper sauce. Cook on HIGH 3 to 4 minutes, stirring after 2 minutes, or until thoroughly heated.

NUTRIENTS PER SERVING			
Calories	285	Fat	5 g
Cholesterol	175 mg	Sodium	839 mg

Favorite recipe from USA Rice Council

Spicy Pasta Del Mar

1	medium onion, diced
1	teaspoon olive oil
1	(10-ounce) can baby clams, drained
2	teaspoons minced garlic
1	(26-ounce) jar HEALTHY CHOICE® Traditional Pasta Sauce
1	teaspoon dried basil leaves
½	teaspoon dried thyme leaves
⅛	teaspoon black pepper
⅛	teaspoon cayenne pepper
½	pound raw medium shrimp, peeled and deveined
½	pound linguini, cooked and drained

In large saucepan, sauté onion in hot oil until tender. Add clams and garlic; cook and stir 1 minute longer. Stir in pasta sauce, basil, thyme, black pepper and cayenne pepper. Heat, stirring occasionally, until mixture comes to a boil. Add shrimp; reduce heat to medium. Cook until shrimp are pink and cooked through. Serve sauce over linguini.   *Makes 6 servings*

NUTRIENTS PER SERVING			
Calories	278	Fat	3 g
Cholesterol	105 mg	Sodium	520 mg

Shrimp Classico

⅔ cup milk

2 tablespoons margarine or butter

1 package (4.8 ounces) PASTA RONI® Herb Sauce with Angel Hair Pasta

1 clove garlic, minced

1 package (10 ounces) frozen chopped spinach, thawed, well drained

1 package (10 ounces) frozen precooked shrimp, thawed, well drained

1 jar (2 ounces) chopped pimiento, drained

1. In 3-quart round microwavable glass casserole, combine 1⅔ cups water, milk and margarine. Microwave, uncovered, on HIGH 4 to 5 minutes or until boiling.

2. Gradually add pasta while stirring. Separate pasta with a fork, if needed. Stir in contents of seasoning packet and garlic.

3. Microwave, uncovered, on HIGH 4 minutes, stirring gently after 2 minutes. Separate pasta with a fork, if needed. Stir in spinach, shrimp and pimiento. Microwave on HIGH 1 to 2 minutes. Sauce will be very thin, but will thicken upon standing.

4. Let stand, uncovered, 2 minutes or until desired consistency. Stir before serving.

Makes 4 servings

NUTRIENTS PER SERVING			
Calories	290	Fat	10 g
Cholesterol	140 mg	Sodium	725 mg

Butterflied Shrimp Parmesan

1½ pounds large shrimp
1 cup (4 ounces) shredded ALPINE LACE® Fat Free
    Pasteurized Process Skim Milk Cheese Product—For
    Parmesan Lovers
¼ cup Italian seasoned dry bread crumbs
2 tablespoons unsalted butter substitute
¾ cup chopped red bell pepper
½ cup thinly sliced green onions
1 tablespoon minced garlic
⅛ teaspoon crushed red pepper flakes or to taste
⅓ cup minced fresh parsley
6 tablespoons 2% low fat milk

1. Peel the shrimp, leaving the tails on. Then butterfly each shrimp by cutting it along the outer curved edge almost all the way through. Open the shrimp up like a book and remove the dark vein. In a small bowl, toss the cheese with the bread crumbs and set aside.

2. In a large nonstick skillet, melt the butter over medium-high heat. Add the bell pepper, green onions, garlic and red pepper flakes and cook for 5 minutes or until soft. Add the shrimp and sauté for 5 minutes or just until the shrimp turn pink and opaque. Stir in the parsley.

3. In a small saucepan, bring the milk just to a boil, then stir into the shrimp mixture. Stir in the cheese mixture and cook until the cheese is melted. Serve immediately.

Makes 4 servings

NUTRIENTS PER SERVING			
Calories	312	Fat	9 g
Cholesterol	281 mg	Sodium	504 mg

Butterflied Shrimp Parmesan

Seafood Paella

Nonstick cooking spray
1   cup finely chopped red bell pepper
⅔   cup finely chopped onion
1   tablespoon minced garlic
½   teaspoon ground turmeric
½   teaspoon paprika
2   teaspoons vegetable flavor bouillon granules
1½ cups uncooked medium grain white rice
1   cup frozen artichoke hearts, thawed, halved
1   pound medium shrimp, peeled and deveined, cut lengthwise
      in half
½   pound sea scallops, cut into quarters
¾   cup frozen baby lima beans, thawed
½   cup frozen sweet peas, thawed

1. Spray large heavy saucepan or deep skillet with cooking spray; heat over medium-high heat until hot. Add bell pepper, onion and garlic; cook and stir 3 minutes or until vegetables are crisp-tender. Stir in turmeric and paprika.

2. Stir 3¼ cups water and bouillon granules into saucepan; bring to a boil over high heat. Stir in rice and artichoke hearts. Cover; reduce heat to medium-low. Simmer 18 minutes, stirring occasionally.

3. Stir shrimp, scallops, beans and peas into saucepan; cover. Simmer 5 minutes or until seafood is opaque and liquid is absorbed. Remove saucepan from heat. Let stand 5 minutes before serving.   *Makes 6 servings*

NUTRIENTS PER SERVING			
Calories	340	Fat	2 g
Cholesterol	132 mg	Sodium	570 mg

Seafood Paella

Shrimp Curry

1¼ pounds raw large shrimp
1 large onion, chopped
½ cup canned light coconut milk
3 cloves garlic, minced
2 tablespoons finely chopped fresh ginger
2 to 3 teaspoons hot curry powder
¼ teaspoon salt
1 can (14½ ounces) diced tomatoes
1 teaspoon cornstarch
2 tablespoons chopped fresh cilantro
3 cups hot cooked rice

1. Peel shrimp, leaving tails attached and reserving shells. Place shells in large saucepan; cover with water. Bring to a boil over high heat. Reduce heat to low; simmer 15 to 20 minutes. Strain shrimp stock and set aside. Discard shells.

2. Spray large skillet with nonstick cooking spray; heat over medium heat. Add onion; cover and cook 5 minutes. Add coconut milk, garlic, ginger, curry powder, salt and ½ cup shrimp stock; bring to a boil. Reduce heat to low and simmer 10 to 15 minutes or until onion is tender.

3. Add shrimp and tomatoes to skillet; return mixture to a simmer. Cook 3 minutes.

4. Stir cornstarch into 1 tablespoon cooled shrimp stock until dissolved. Add mixture to skillet with cilantro; simmer 1 to 2 minutes or just until slightly thickened, stirring occasionally. Serve over rice. Garnish with carrot and lime slices, if desired. *Makes 6 servings*

NUTRIENTS PER SERVING			
Calories	219	Fat	2 g
Cholesterol	145 mg	Sodium	369 mg

Angel Hair Pasta with Seafood Sauce

½ pound firm whitefish, such as sea bass, monkfish or grouper
2 teaspoons olive oil
½ cup chopped onion
2 cloves garlic, minced
3 pounds fresh plum tomatoes, seeded and chopped
¼ cup chopped fresh basil
2 tablespoons chopped fresh oregano
1 teaspoon red pepper flakes
½ teaspoon sugar
2 bay leaves
½ pound fresh bay scallops or shucked oysters
8 ounces uncooked angel hair pasta
2 tablespoons chopped fresh parsley

1. Cut whitefish into ¾-inch pieces. Set aside.

2. Heat oil in large nonstick skillet over medium heat; add onion and garlic. Cook and stir 3 minutes or until onion is tender. Reduce heat to low; add tomatoes, basil, oregano, crushed red pepper flakes, sugar and bay leaves. Cook, uncovered, 15 minutes, stirring occasionally.

3. Add whitefish and scallops. Cook, uncovered, 3 to 4 minutes or until fish flakes easily when tested with fork and scallops are opaque. Remove bay leaves; discard. Set seafood sauce aside.

4. Cook pasta according to package directions, omitting salt. Drain well.

5. Combine pasta with seafood sauce in large serving bowl. Mix well. Sprinkle with parsley. Serve immediately.   *Makes 6 servings*

NUTRIENTS PER SERVING			
Calories	272	Fat	5 g
Cholesterol	31 mg	Sodium	134 mg

Angel Hair Pasta with Seafood Sauce

SMUCKER'S® Mandarin Shrimp and Vegetable Stir Fry

1 cup SMUCKER'S® Orange Marmalade
3 tablespoons soy sauce
2 tablespoons white vinegar
2 teaspoons hot pepper sauce
4½ teaspoons cornstarch
2 tablespoons vegetable oil
1 tablespoon fresh ginger, chopped
1 tablespoon garlic, chopped
24 fresh jumbo shrimp, peeled and deveined
1 red bell pepper, chopped
1 yellow or green bell pepper, chopped
3 cups broccoli florets (about 1 bunch)
½ cup water
1 cup scallions, chopped (about 1 bunch)

Combine the Smucker's® Orange Marmalade, soy sauce, vinegar, hot pepper sauce and cornstarch in a small bowl. Stir to dissolve the cornstarch and set aside.

Place a large skillet or wok over high heat. Heat the pan for 1 minute, then add the vegetable oil. Heat the oil for 30 seconds, then add the ginger, garlic and shrimp. Stir-fry for 2 to 3 minutes until the shrimp begin to turn rosy pink in color. Remove the shrimp from the pan and set aside.

Add the peppers and broccoli florets to the pan and cook on high heat for 1 minute. Add the water; cover and reduce heat to medium. Cook the vegetables 4 to 5 minutes or until tender.

Uncover pan and increase the heat to high. Add shrimp and Smucker's® Orange Marmalade mixture. Cook shrimp for another 2 minutes until sauce is thickened and the shrimp are completely cooked. Correct seasoning with salt and fresh ground black pepper as needed.

Stir in the scallions and serve with boiled rice. *Makes 4 to 6 servings*

NUTRIENTS PER SERVING			
Calories	278	Fat	6 g
Cholesterol	62 mg	Sodium	633 mg

Linguine with White Clam Sauce

2 tablespoons CRISCO® Savory Seasonings
   Roasted Garlic Flavor oil
2 cloves garlic, minced
2 cans (6½ ounces each) chopped clams, undrained
½ cup chopped fresh parsley
¼ cup dry white wine
1 teaspoon dried basil leaves
1 pound linguine, cooked (without salt or fat) and well drained

1. Heat oil and garlic in medium skillet on medium heat.

2. Drain clams, reserving liquid. Add reserved liquid and parsley to skillet. Reduce heat to low. Simmer 3 minutes, stirring occasionally.

3. Add clams, wine and basil. Simmer 5 minutes, stirring occasionally. Add to hot linguine. Toss lightly to coat. *Makes 8 servings*

NUTRIENTS PER SERVING			
Calories	185	Fat	5 g
Cholesterol	30 mg	Sodium	55 mg

Chilled Poached Salmon with Cucumber Sauce

1 cup water
½ teaspoon chicken or fish bouillon granules
⅛ teaspoon pepper
4 fresh or thawed frozen pink salmon fillets (about 6 ounces each)
½ cup chopped seeded peeled cucumber
⅓ cup plain low-fat yogurt
2 tablespoons sliced green onion
2 tablespoons nonfat salad dressing or mayonnaise
1 tablespoon chopped fresh cilantro
1 teaspoon Dijon mustard
2 cups shredded lettuce

Combine water, bouillon granules and pepper in large skillet. Bring to a boil over high heat. Carefully place salmon in skillet; return just to a boil. Reduce heat to medium-low. Cover and simmer 8 to 10 minutes or until salmon flakes easily when tested with fork. Remove salmon. Cover and refrigerate.

Meanwhile, combine cucumber, yogurt, onion, salad dressing, cilantro and mustard in small bowl. Cover and refrigerate. Place chilled salmon fillets on lettuce-lined plates. Spoon sauce over salmon. *Makes 4 servings*

NUTRIENTS PER SERVING			
Calories	223	Fat	6 g
Cholesterol	89 mg	Sodium	322 mg

Chilled Poached Salmon with Cucumber Sauce

No-Fuss Tuna Quiche

1   unbaked 9-inch deep-dish pastry shell
1½ cups low-fat milk
3   extra large eggs
⅓   cup chopped green onions
1   tablespoon chopped drained pimiento
1   teaspoon dried basil leaves
½   teaspoon salt
1   can (6 ounces) STARKIST® Tuna, drained and flaked
½   cup (2 ounces) shredded low-fat Cheddar cheese
8   spears (4 inches each) broccoli

Preheat oven to 450°F. Bake pastry shell for 5 minutes; remove to rack to cool. *Reduce oven temperature to 325°F.* For filling, in large bowl whisk together milk and eggs. Stir in onions, pimiento, basil and salt. Fold in tuna and cheese. Pour into prebaked pastry shell. Bake at 325°F for 30 minutes.

Meanwhile, in a saucepan steam broccoli spears over simmering water for 5 minutes. Drain; set aside. After 30 minutes baking time, arrange broccoli spears, spoke-fashion, over quiche. Bake 25 to 35 minutes more or until a knife inserted 2 inches from center comes out clean. Let stand for 5 minutes. Cut into 8 wedges, centering a broccoli spear in each wedge.   *Makes 8 servings*

Note: If desired, 1 cup chopped broccoli may be added to the filling before baking.

NUTRIENTS PER SERVING			
Calories	226	Fat	10 g
Cholesterol	95 mg	Sodium	461 mg

202

Southern Breaded Catfish

⅓ cup pecan halves
¼ cup cornmeal
2 tablespoons all-purpose flour
1 teaspoon paprika
¼ teaspoon ground red pepper
2 egg whites
4 catfish fillets (about 1 pound)
4 cups cooked rice

1. Place pecans in food processor or blender; process until finely chopped. Combine pecans, cornmeal, flour, paprika and ground red pepper in shallow bowl.

2. Beat egg whites in small bowl with wire whisk until foamy. Dip catfish fillets in pecan mixture, then in egg whites, then again in pecan mixture. Place fillets on plate; cover and refrigerate at least 15 minutes.

3. Spray large nonstick skillet with nonstick cooking spray; heat over medium-high heat. Place catfish fillets in single layer in skillet.

4. Cook fillets 2 minutes per side or until golden brown. Serve over rice. Serve with vegetables and garnish, if desired. *Makes 4 servings*

NUTRIENTS PER SERVING			
Calories	297	Fat	8 g
Cholesterol	65 mg	Sodium	76 mg

Southern Breaded Catfish

Snapper Veracruz

Nonstick cooking spray
1   teaspoon olive oil
¼   large onion, thinly sliced
⅓   cup low sodium fish or vegetable broth, defatted*
2   cloves garlic, minced
1   cup GUILTLESS GOURMET® Salsa (mild, medium or hot)
20 ounces fresh red snapper, tilapia, sea bass or halibut fillets

Preheat oven to 400°F. Coat baking dish with cooking spray. (Dish needs to be large enough for fish to fit snugly together.) Heat oil in large nonstick skillet over medium heat until hot. Add onion; cook and stir until onion is translucent. When skillet becomes dry, stir in 3 tablespoons broth. Add garlic; cook and stir 1 minute more. Stir in remaining broth and salsa. Bring mixture to a boil. Reduce heat to low; simmer about 2 minutes or until heated through.

Wash fish thoroughly; pat dry with paper towels. Place in prepared baking dish, overlapping thin edges to obtain an overall equal thickness. Pour and spread salsa mixture over fish.

Bake 15 minutes or until fish turns opaque and flakes easily when tested with fork. Serve hot.   *Makes 4 servings*

*To defat broth, simply chill the canned broth thoroughly. Open the can and use a spoon to lift out any solid fat floating on the surface of the broth.

NUTRIENTS PER SERVING			
Calories	184	Fat	3 g
Cholesterol	52 mg	Sodium	353 mg

Snapper Veracruz

Golden Apple Stuffed Fillets

1 cup grated, peeled Golden Delicious apple
½ cup grated carrot
½ cup minced green onions
2 tablespoons fresh lemon juice
¼ teaspoon ground ginger
¼ teaspoon ground mustard
¼ teaspoon salt
¼ teaspoon ground black pepper
⅛ teaspoon dried thyme
4 sole, cod or other white fish fillets (4 to 5 ounces each)
¼ cup chicken broth or water

1. Heat oven to 400°F; lightly oil small roasting pan. In medium bowl, combine apple, carrot, green onions, lemon juice, ginger, mustard, salt, pepper and thyme; mix well.

2. Spread apple mixture evenly over length of fillets; carefully roll up from shorter ends. Place stuffed fillets, seam side down, in oiled pan. Pour broth over rolled fillets; cover with aluminum foil and bake 10 to 15 minutes or until fish is opaque and barely flakes. *Makes 4 servings*

Microwave Directions: Prepare apple stuffing mixture and roll up fillets as above. Place stuffed fillets, seam side down, in oiled microwave-safe dish. Pour broth over rolled fillets; cover with waxed paper and microwave on HIGH (100% power) 5 to 7 minutes or until fish is opaque and barely flakes. (If microwave does not have carousel, rotate dish halfway through cooking.)

NUTRIENTS PER SERVING			
Calories	176	Fat	2 g
Cholesterol	75 mg	Sodium	314 mg

Favorite recipe from Washington Apple Commission

Ragoût of Tuna

2   cloves garlic, minced, divided
1   or 2 sprigs fresh mint, chopped *or* 1 teaspoon dried mint
    leaves
½   to 1 teaspoon salt, divided
    Pepper to taste
2   to 2½ pounds fresh tuna or swordfish
2   teaspoons olive oil
½   cup dry white wine
2   medium onions, thinly sliced
1   teaspoon sugar
1   pound ripe tomatoes, coarsely chopped
1   cup hot water
4   cups hot cooked noodles or rice (optional)

Combine half of garlic, mint, half of salt and pepper in small bowl. Make about 12 cuts into sides of fish. Insert garlic mixture into each cut. Heat oil over medium-high heat in large nonstick skillet; add fish and brown on both sides. Pour wine over fish; continue cooking, basting with liquid, until wine has completely evaporated, about 5 minutes. Transfer fish to warm casserole.

Add remaining garlic and onions to skillet. Sprinkle with sugar and remaining salt; cook over low heat, about 5 minutes. Return fish to skillet. Add tomatoes and hot water; simmer until fish is cooked through and sauce thickens. To serve, pour sauce over fish and serve remaining sauce with noodles or rice, if desired.

Makes 6 servings

NUTRIENTS PER SERVING			
Calories	224	Fat	3 g
Cholesterol	69 mg	Sodium	243 mg

Favorite recipe from **The Sugar Association, Inc.**

Ragoût of Tuna

208

Microwave Flounder with Carrots

1 pound carrots, julienned (about 4 large)
2 tablespoons minced parsley
1 teaspoon olive oil
⅛ teaspoon salt
⅛ teaspoon pepper
4 flounder fillets* (4 to 5 ounces each)
2 teaspoons coarse-grain Dijon mustard
1 teaspoon honey

Combine carrots, parsley, oil, salt and pepper in 11×7×2-inch microwave-safe baking dish. Cover with waxed paper. Microwave at HIGH (100% power) 5 minutes, stirring once.

Fold thin fillets in half to give all fillets even thickness. Place fillets over carrots in corners of dish with thick parts toward outside and thin parts toward center. Combine mustard and honey; spread over fillets.

Cover with waxed paper. Microwave at HIGH 2 minutes. Rotate fillets, placing cooked parts toward the center; continue to cook 1 to 3 minutes longer or just until fish flakes easily when tested with a fork. Let stand, covered, 2 minutes. Arrange fish and carrots on 4 warm plates. *Makes 4 servings*

*Or, substitute other fish fillets, such as tilapia, sole, cod, catfish, halibut, ocean perch, trout, orange roughy or pollock.

NUTRIENTS PER SERVING			
(4 ounces)			
Calories	170	Fat	3 g
Cholesterol	54 mg	Sodium	229 mg

Favorite recipe from **National Fisheries Institute**

Microwave Flounder with Carrots

Salmon Steaks with Lemon Dill Sauce

½ cup finely chopped red onion
2 teaspoons FLEISCHMANN'S® Margarine
2 tablespoons all-purpose flour
1⅓ cups skim milk
½ cup EGG BEATERS® Healthy Real Egg Product
2 teaspoons grated lemon pccl
¼ cup lemon juice
2 teaspoons dried dill weed
8 (½-inch-thick) salmon steaks (2 pounds)
Fresh dill sprigs, for garnish

In small saucepan, over low heat, sauté onion in margarine until tender-crisp. Stir in flour; cook for 1 minute. Over medium heat, gradually stir in milk; cook, stirring until mixture thickens and boils. Boil, stirring constantly, for 1 minute; remove from heat. Whisk in Egg Beaters®, lemon peel, lemon juice and dried dill; return to heat. Cook, stirring constantly until thickened. *Do not boil.*

Meanwhile, grill or broil salmon steaks for 3 to 5 minutes on each side or until fish flakes easily when tested with fork. Top with sauce. Garnish with dill sprigs.   *Makes 8 servings*

Prep time: 15 minutes
Cook time: 15 minutes

NUTRIENTS PER SERVING			
Calories	255	Fat	11 g
Cholesterol	83 mg	Sodium	118 mg

Salmon Steak with Lemon Dill Sauce

Wisconsin Tuna Cakes with Lemon-Dill Sauce

    1 can (12 ounces) STARKIST® Tuna, drained and finely flaked
   ¾ cup seasoned bread crumbs
   ¼ cup minced green onions
   2 tablespoons chopped drained pimientos
   1 egg
   ½ cup low-fat milk
   ½ teaspoon grated lemon peel
   2 tablespoons margarine or butter

LEMON–DILL SAUCE
   ¼ cup chicken broth
   1 tablespoon lemon juice
   ¼ teaspoon dried dill weed
       Hot steamed shredded zucchini and carrots
       Lemon slices

214

In large bowl, toss together tuna, bread crumbs, onions and pimientos. In small bowl, beat together egg and milk; stir in lemon peel. Stir into tuna mixture; toss until moistened. With lightly floured hands, shape into eight 4-inch patties.

In large nonstick skillet, melt margarine. Fry patties, a few at a time, until golden brown on both sides, about 3 minutes per side. Place on ovenproof platter in 300°F oven until ready to serve.

For Lemon-Dill Sauce, in small saucepan, heat broth, lemon juice and dill. Serve tuna cakes with zucchini and carrots; spoon sauce over cakes. Garnish with lemon slices.   *Makes 4 servings*

NUTRIENTS PER SERVING			
(2 patties plus 1 tablespoon sauce)			
Calories	278	Fat	10 g
Cholesterol	85 mg	Sodium	576 mg

Wisconsin Tuna Cakes with Lemon-Dill Sauce

Salads

• • • • • • • • • •

Mediterranean Pasta Salad

1 package (8 ounces) refrigerated or frozen cheese tortellini
1 package (9 ounces) DOLE® Italian Style Vegetables
1 can (8 ounces) DOLE® Pineapple Chunks
2 tablespoons balsamic or red wine vinegar
1 tablespoon olive or vegetable oil
¼ pound fresh link turkey sausage, cooked, drained and sliced
1 medium DOLE® Red, Yellow or Green Bell Pepper, cubed

• **Prepare** tortellini according to package directions, adding Italian Style Vegetables (reserve seasoning packet) during last 2 minutes of cooking. Meanwhile, prepare dressing.

• **Drain** pineapple; reserve ¼ cup juice.

• **Combine** reserved juice, vinegar, oil and tomato basil seasoning packet from vegetable package in large serving bowl.

• **Drain** tortellini and vegetables. Add tortellini, vegetables, sausage, bell pepper and pineapple to dressing; toss well to evenly coat. Serve at room temperature or chilled. Toss before serving.   *Makes 6 servings*

Prep time: 10 minutes
Cook time: 20 minutes

NUTRIENTS PER SERVING			
Calories	184	Fat	5 g
Cholesterol	19 mg	Sodium	290 mg

Hot to Go Thai Salad

¾ pound sirloin steak
⅓ cup vegetable oil, divided
⅓ cup rice vinegar*
¼ cup reduced-sodium soy sauce
1 fresh jalapeño or serrano pepper, finely chopped, divided
2 cloves garlic, minced
1 tablespoon minced fresh gingerroot
½ teaspoon red pepper flakes
1 (9-ounce) package French-style green beans, thawed and
    drained
2 carrots, halved and thinly sliced
1 cucumber, peeled, seeded and sliced
4 cups cooked brown rice
  Chopped fresh mint leaves (optional)

Partially freeze steak; slice across grain into ¼-inch strips. Place in large bowl.
Combine all but 1 tablespoon oil, vinegar, soy sauce, ½ of the jalapeño, garlic,
gingerroot and red pepper flakes in small bowl. Pour mixture over beef;
marinate 1 hour. Drain beef; discard marinade. Heat remaining 1 tablespoon oil
in large skillet over medium-high heat until hot. Add beef and remaining
jalapeño; cook 3 to 5 minutes or until no longer pink. Combine beef, liquid from
skillet, beans, carrots, cucumber and rice in large bowl. Toss to coat. Sprinkle
with mint, if desired.   *Makes 6 servings*

*White wine vinegar may be substituted.

NUTRIENTS PER SERVING			
Calories	296	Fat	8 g
Cholesterol	38 mg	Sodium	565 mg

Favorite recipe from **USA Rice Council**

Hot to Go Thai Salad

Three-Pepper Tuna Salad

     2 cups thinly sliced zucchini
    ½ cup red bell pepper strips
    ½ cup green bell pepper strips
    ½ cup yellow bell pepper strips
     1 cup cherry tomatoes, halved
     1 can (6 ounces) solid albacore tuna packed in water, drained
    ¼ cup chopped green onions with tops
    ¼ cup chopped fresh basil
    2½ tablespoons red wine vinegar
     1 tablespoon olive oil
    ½ teaspoon minced fresh garlic
    ½ teaspoon fresh marjoram
    ⅛ teaspoon ground black pepper

1. Pour ¾ cup water into medium saucepan. Add zucchini and bell pepper strips. Steam vegetables about 10 minutes or until crisp-tender. Remove from heat; drain any excess water. Transfer to serving bowl. Add tomatoes, tuna, green onions and basil.

2. Combine vinegar, oil, garlic, marjoram and black pepper in jar or bottle with tight-fitting lid; shake well. Pour dressing over vegetable mixture; mix well. Garnish as desired.   *Makes 4 servings*

NUTRIENTS PER SERVING			
Calories	134	Fat	5 g
Cholesterol	18 mg	Sodium	175 mg

Three-Pepper Tuna Salad

Healthy Chef's Salad

PEPPER CRÈME DRESSING

- ⅔ cup reduced calorie mayonnaise
- ⅔ cup fat free sour cream
- ⅓ cup bottled chili sauce
- ⅓ cup chopped red bell pepper
- ¼ cup minced chives or green onions
- 2 tablespoons fresh lemon juice
- ½ teaspoon freshly ground black pepper

CHEF'S SALAD

- 12 cups washed and coarsely torn mixed salad greens (leaf lettuce, romaine and endive)
- 1 small cucumber, halved lengthwise and thinly sliced
- ⅓ cup finely chopped green onions, divided
- 1 cup cooked corn kernels
- 1 cup cooked green peas
- 3 cups peeled and grated carrots
- 4 medium-size ripe tomatoes, cut into wedges
- 12 ounces skinless roasted turkey breast, cut into thin strips
- 6 ounces ALPINE LACE® Boneless Cooked Ham, cut into thin strips
- 6 ounces ALPINE LACE® Reduced Fat Swiss Cheese, cut into thin strips
- 6 ounces roast beef, cut into thin strips (optional)
- 2 large eggs, hard-cooked, peeled and thinly sliced (optional)

1. To make the Pepper Crème Dressing: In a medium-size bowl, whisk all of the dressing ingredients together until well blended.

2. To make the Chef's Salad: In a large, shallow salad bowl, toss the greens, cucumber, half of the green onions, the corn and peas. Mound the carrots in

continued on page 224

Healthy Chef's Salad

Healthy Chef's Salad, continued

the center and arrange the tomatoes around the edge. In a spoke design, alternately arrange on the greens the turkey, ham and cheese, plus the beef and eggs, if you wish. Sprinkle with the remaining green onions and serve with the dressing.   *Makes 10 luncheon servings or 6 supper servings*

NUTRIENTS PER SERVING			
Calories	262	Fat	10 g
Cholesterol	49 mg	Sodium	515 mg

Smoked Turkey & Fruit Salad

1   package (16 ounces) DOLE® Classic Blend Salad
1   can (11 ounces) DOLE® Mandarin Oranges, drained
4   ounces deli-sliced smoked turkey or chicken, cut into ½-inch
      slices
½   cup DOLE® Golden or Seedless Raisins
½   cup fat free or light ranch salad dressing
1   can (20 ounces) DOLE® Pineapple Slices, drained and cut in
      half

• **Toss** together salad, mandarin oranges, turkey and raisins in large bowl. Pour in dressing; toss well to evenly coat.

• **Spoon** salad onto large serving platter. Arrange halved pineapple slices around salad.   *Makes 4 servings*

Prep time: 15 minutes

NUTRIENTS PER SERVING			
Calories	160	Fat	1 g
Cholesterol	8 mg	Sodium	413 mg

Honey-Dijon Salad with Shrimp

8 cups torn romaine lettuce leaves
1 pound large shrimp, cleaned and cooked
3 cups sliced mushrooms
2 cups sliced carrots
½ cup EGG BEATERS® Healthy Real Egg Product
¼ cup corn oil
¼ cup REGINA® White Wine Vinegar
¼ cup GREY POUPON® Dijon Mustard
¼ cup honey
2 cups plain croutons, optional
Carrot curls, for garnish

In large bowl, combine lettuce, shrimp, mushrooms and sliced carrots; set aside.

In small bowl, whisk together Egg Beaters®, oil, vinegar, mustard and honey until well blended. To serve, pour dressing over salad, tossing until well coated. Top with croutons, if desired. Garnish with carrot curls.   *Makes 8 servings*

Prep time: 25 minutes

NUTRIENTS PER SERVING			
Calories	252	Fat	9 g
Cholesterol	111 mg	Sodium	538 mg

Santa Fe Chicken Pasta Salad

12 ounces uncooked spiral pasta
 2 cups cooked chicken breast cubes
½ cup chopped green onions
 1 medium zucchini or yellow squash, cut in half lengthwise,
      then sliced crosswise
 1 cup GUILTLESS GOURMET® Green Tomatillo Salsa
½ cup sliced black olives
 1 cup drained and coarsely chopped artichoke hearts
      Lettuce leaves
      Fresh dill sprigs (optional)

Cook pasta according to package directions; drain. Place pasta in large
nonmetal bowl; add chicken, onions, zucchini, tomatillo salsa, olives and
artichoke hearts. Toss lightly. Refrigerate at least 6 hours before serving.

To serve, line serving platter with lettuce leaves. Top with pasta mixture.
Garnish with dill, if desired.   *Makes 4 servings*

NUTRIENTS PER SERVING			
Calories	413	Fat	5 g
Cholesterol	45 mg	Sodium	429 mg

Tossed Rice Salad with Balsamic Vinaigrette

½ cup unsweetened orange juice
3 tablespoons vegetable oil, divided
2 tablespoons balsamic vinegar or red wine vinegar
2 teaspoons honey
1 teaspoon grated orange peel
1 teaspoon Dijon mustard
¾ pound pork tenderloin
3 cups cooked brown rice
1 pint fresh strawberries, sliced
1 cup seedless red or green grapes, halved
   Lettuce leaves

Combine orange juice, 2 tablespoons oil, vinegar, honey, orange peel and mustard in large bowl. Cut pork into ¼-inch slices. Cut each slice into julienne strips. Add pork to marinade; stir to coat. Marinate in refrigerator 4 hours or overnight. Drain pork, reserving marinade. Transfer marinade to small saucepan; heat to boiling. Boil 1 minute; remove from heat. Heat remaining 1 tablespoon oil in large skillet over medium-high heat until hot. Cook pork, stirring, until no longer pink, about 5 to 7 minutes. Drain liquid. Remove from heat; cool.

Combine pork, rice, strawberries and grapes in large bowl. Pour marinade over salad; toss well. Serve immediately on lettuce leaves.   *Makes 6 servings*

NUTRIENTS PER SERVING			
Calories	299	Fat	10 g
Cholesterol	40 mg	Sodium	250 mg

Favorite recipe from **USA Rice Council**

Tossed Rice Salad with Balsamic Vinaigrette

Nacho Salad

3 ounces (about 60) GUILTLESS GOURMET® Unsalted Baked
   Tortilla Chips
2 teaspoons water
½ cup GUILTLESS GOURMET® Black Bean Dip (mild or spicy)
½ cup GUILTLESS GOURMET® Nacho Dip (mild or spicy)
4 cups shredded romaine lettuce
2 medium tomatoes (red or yellow), chopped
½ cup GUILTLESS GOURMET® Green Tomatillo Salsa

Divide and spread tortilla chips among 4 plates. Stir water into bean dip in
small microwave-safe bowl or small saucepan. Microwave bean dip on HIGH
(100% power) 2 to 3 minutes or heat over medium heat until warm. Heat nacho
dip in separate small microwave-safe bowl or small saucepan as directed above.
Evenly drizzle heated dips over tortilla chips. Sprinkle lettuce and tomatoes
evenly over tortilla chips. To serve, spoon 2 tablespoons tomatillo salsa over
each salad. *Makes 4 servings*

NUTRIENTS PER SERVING			
Calories	171	Fat	<1 g
Cholesterol	0 mg	Sodium	445 mg

Nacho Salad

Spicy Orzo and Black Bean Salad

2 tablespoons olive oil
2 tablespoons minced jalapeño pepper, divided*
1 teaspoon chili powder
¾ cup uncooked orzo pasta
1 cup frozen mixed vegetables
1 can (16 ounces) black beans, rinsed and drained
2 thin slices red onion
¼ cup chopped cilantro
¼ cup fresh lime juice
¼ cup fresh lemon juice
4 cups washed and torn spinach leaves
2 tablespoons crumbled blue cheese (optional)

1. Combine oil, 1 tablespoon jalapeño and chili powder in medium bowl.

2. Bring 6 cups water and remaining 1 tablespoon jalapeño to a boil in large saucepan. Add orzo. Cook 10 to 12 minutes or until tender; drain. Rinse in cold water; drain.

3. Place frozen vegetables in small microwavable container. Cover and microwave at HIGH 3 minutes or until hot. Cover and let stand 5 minutes.

4. Add orzo, vegetables, black beans, onion, cilantro, lime juice and lemon juice to oil mixture in bowl. Divide spinach evenly among serving plates. Top with orzo and bean mixture. Sprinkle with blue cheese and garnish with fresh cilantro, if desired.   *Makes 4 servings*

*Jalapeño peppers can sting and irritate the skin; wear rubber gloves when handling peppers and do not touch eyes. Wash hands after handling jalapeño peppers.

NUTRIENTS PER SERVING			
Calories	356	Fat	9 g
Cholesterol	0 mg	Sodium	467 mg

Spicy Orzo and Black Bean Salad

Spinach-Tomato Salad

1   package (8 ounces) DOLE® Complete Spinach Salad
2   medium tomatoes, halved and cut into thin wedges
½   medium cucumber, thinly sliced
½   small onion, thinly sliced
1   can (14 to 16 ounces) low-sodium kidney or garbanzo beans,
    drained

• **Toss** spinach, croutons and bacon from salad bag with tomatoes, cucumber, onion and beans in medium serving bowl.

• **Pour** dressing from packet over salad; toss to coat evenly.

Makes 4 servings

Prep time: 10 minutes

NUTRIENTS PER SERVING			
Calories	210	Fat	6 g
Cholesterol	0 mg	Sodium	423 mg

Spinach-Tomato Salad

Salad Primavera

6 cups romaine lettuce, washed, torn into bite-sized pieces
1 package (9 ounces) frozen artichoke hearts, thawed, drained,
    cut into bite-sized pieces
1 cup chopped watercress
1 orange, peeled, separated into segments, cut into halves
½ cup chopped red bell pepper
¼ cup chopped green onions with tops
    Citrus-Caper Dressing (recipe follows)
2 tablespoons freshly grated Parmesan cheese

1. Combine lettuce, artichoke hearts, watercress, orange segments, bell pepper and green onions in large bowl. Prepare Citrus-Caper Dressing. Add dressing to lettuce mixture. Mix well. Sprinkle with Parmesan before serving.

Makes 8 servings

CITRUS–CAPER DRESSING

⅓ cup orange juice
¼ cup white wine vinegar
2 tablespoons chopped fresh parsley
2 teaspoons Dijon mustard
¼ teaspoon olive oil
1 tablespoon minced capers
1 teaspoon sugar
1 teaspoon minced fresh garlic
¼ teaspoon ground black pepper

1. Combine all ingredients in jar or bottle with tight-fitting lid; shake well. Refrigerate until ready to serve. Shake well before using.

Makes ½ cup dressing

NUTRIENTS PER SERVING			
Calories	55	Fat	1 g
Cholesterol	1 mg	Sodium	102 mg

Salad Primavera

Vegetable Potato Salad

½ cup cider vinegar
¼ cup CRISCO® Oil
½ teaspoon prepared mustard
½ teaspoon salt
¼ teaspoon pepper
2¾ pounds unpeeled medium red potatoes
3 medium carrots, cut into thin 2-inch sticks
3 ribs celery, sliced
3 green onions with tops, chopped
6 radishes, sliced
4 tomatoes, quartered

1. Combine vinegar, oil, mustard, salt and pepper in container with tight-fitting lid. Shake well.

2. Cook potatoes just until tender. Cool 5 minutes. Cut into bite-size pieces. Combine in large salad bowl with carrots, celery, onions and radishes. Shake dressing. Pour over salad. Toss to mix well. Serve immediately or refrigerate. Top with tomato wedges. *Makes 8 servings*

NUTRIENTS PER SERVING			
Calories	225	Fat	7 g
Cholesterol	0 mg	Sodium	175 mg

Marinated Vegetable Spinach Salad

Mustard-Tarragon Marinade (recipe follows)
8 ounces fresh mushrooms, quartered
2 slices purple onion, separated into rings
16 cherry tomatoes, halved
4 cups fresh spinach leaves, washed and stems removed
3 slices (3 ounces) SARGENTO® Preferred Light Sliced
    Mozzarella Cheese, cut into julienne strips
    Freshly ground black pepper

Prepare Mustard-Tarragon Marinade; set aside. Place mushrooms, onion and tomatoes in bowl. Toss with marinade and let stand 15 minutes. Arrange spinach on 4 individual plates. Divide marinated vegetables among plates and top each salad with ¼ of cheese. Serve with freshly ground black pepper, if desired.   *Makes 4 servings*

MUSTARD–TARRAGON MARINADE

3 tablespoons red wine vinegar
1 tablespoon Dijon-style mustard
½ tablespoon dried tarragon
2 tablespoons olive oil

Combine first 3 ingredients in small bowl. Slowly whisk oil into mixture until slightly thickened.

NUTRIENTS PER SERVING			
Calories	147	Fat	10 g
Cholesterol	7 mg	Sodium	252 mg

Roasted Red Pepper, Corn & Garbanzo Bean Salad

        2 cans (15 ounces each) garbanzo beans
        1 jar (11.5 ounces) GUILTLESS GOURMET® Roasted Red
             Pepper Salsa
        1 cup frozen whole kernel corn, thawed and drained
        ½ cup GUILTLESS GOURMET® Green Tomatillo Salsa
        2 green onions, thinly sliced
        8 lettuce leaves
            Fresh tomato wedges and sunflower sprouts (optional)

Rinse and drain beans well; place in 2-quart casserole dish. Add roasted red
pepper salsa, corn, tomatillo salsa and onions; stir to combine. Cover and
refrigerate 1 hour or up to 24 hours.

To serve, line serving platter with lettuce. Spoon bean mixture over top.
Garnish with tomatoes and sprouts, if desired.   *Makes 8 servings*

NUTRIENTS PER SERVING			
Calories	174	Fat	2 g
Cholesterol	0 mg	Sodium	268 mg

Roasted Red Pepper, Corn & Garbanzo Bean Salad

Minted Fruit Rice Salad

⅔ cup DOLE® Pineapple Orange Juice, Mandarin Tangerine
    Juice or Pineapple Juice
⅓ cup water
1 cup uncooked instant rice
1 can (11 ounces) DOLE® Mandarin Oranges, drained
1 can (8 ounces) DOLE® Crushed Pineapple
½ cup chopped cucumber
⅓ cup chopped DOLE® Red Onion
3 tablespoons chopped fresh mint

• **Combine** juice and water in medium saucepan. Bring to boil. Stir in rice.
Remove from heat; cover. Let stand 10 minutes.

• **Stir** together rice, drained mandarin oranges, undrained pineapple,
cucumber, onion and mint in medium serving bowl. Serve at room temperature
or chilled.   *Makes 4 servings*

Prep time: 5 minutes
Cook time: 15 minutes

NUTRIENTS PER SERVING			
Calories	106	Fat	0 g
Cholesterol	0 mg	Sodium	4 mg

Minted Fruit Rice Salad

Cool Summer Gazpacho Salad

1 large DOLE® Fresh Pineapple
2 cups chopped tomatoes, drained
1 large cucumber, halved lengthwise and thinly sliced
¼ cup chopped DOLE® Green Onions
¼ cup red wine vinegar
4 teaspoons olive or vegetable oil
½ teaspoon dried basil leaves, crushed

• **Twist** off crown from pineapple. Cut pineapple in quarters lengthwise. Remove fruit. Core and dice fruit. Drain fruit.

• **Stir** together pineapple and remaining ingredients in large bowl. Cover; chill 1 hour or overnight to blend flavors. Stir before serving.   *Makes 10 servings*

Prep time: 20 minutes
Chill time: 1 hour

NUTRIENTS PER SERVING			
Calories	68	Fat	2 g
Cholesterol	0 mg	Sodium	5 mg

Cool Summer Gazpacho Salad

Summer Fruit Salad

2 cups cooked rice, cooled to room temperature
½ cup quartered strawberries
½ cup grape halves
½ cup pineapple tidbits
2 kiwifruit, sliced into quarters
½ cup banana slices
¼ cup pineapple juice
2 tablespoons plain nonfat yogurt
1 tablespoon honey
Lettuce leaves

Combine rice and fruit in large bowl. Blend pineapple juice, yogurt, and honey in small bowl. Pour over rice mixture; toss lightly. Serve on lettuce leaves.

Makes 4 servings

NUTRIENTS PER SERVING			
Calories	239	Fat	1 g
Cholesterol	1 mg	Sodium	396 mg

Favorite recipe from USA Rice Council

Summer Fruit Salad

Southwest Salsa Dressing

⅔ cup mild salsa*
2 tablespoons plain nonfat yogurt
4 teaspoons sugar
2 teaspoons chopped fresh cilantro (optional)

In a small bowl stir all ingredients together. Or, blend ingredients in a food processor for a smoother dressing. Chill or serve immediately over green salad, chicken or turkey salad, taco salad or seafood salad.   *Makes 4 servings*

*For a hotter and spicier dressing, use medium or hot salsa.

NUTRIENTS PER SERVING			
(approximately 2 tablespoons)			
Calories	30	Fat	<1 g
Cholesterol	226 mg	Sodium	226 mg

Favorite recipe from **The Sugar Association, Inc.**

Mock Blue Cheese Dressing

¾ cup buttermilk
¼ cup low-fat cottage cheese
2 tablespoons blue cheese, crumbled
2 teaspoons sugar
1 teaspoon lemon juice
¼ teaspoon celery seed
⅛ teaspoon pepper
⅛ teaspoon salt
4 drops hot sauce

In a blender or food processor blend all ingredients. Chill and serve over green salad. *Makes 6 servings*

NUTRIENTS PER SERVING			
(approximately 2 tablespoons)			
Calories	22	Fat	1 g
Cholesterol	3 mg	Sodium	148 mg

Favorite recipe from **The Sugar Association, Inc.**

Microwave or Roasted Bell Pepper Dressing

   1   green or red bell pepper
 ½   cup buttermilk
   2   teaspoons sugar
   1   teaspoon fresh parsley (optional)
 ¾   teaspoon lemon juice
 ¼   teaspoon paprika
 ⅛   teaspoon salt
 ⅛   teaspoon pepper
 ⅛   teaspoon onion powder

Microwave bell pepper for 5 minutes on HIGH (100% power) until tender (cooking time may vary depending on microwave). Or, roast pepper at 375°F for 20 to 25 minutes until tender. Cut pepper in half and remove seeds. Pat dry with paper towel. In a blender or food processor blend all ingredients thoroughly. Chill and serve over green salad. *Makes 6 servings*

NUTRIENTS PER SERVING			
(approximately 2 tablespoons)			
Calories	21	Fat	<1 g
Cholesterol	1 mg	Sodium	67 mg

Favorite recipe from **The Sugar Association, Inc.**

Creamy Garlic Dressing

12 ounces (2 cartons) ALPINE LACE® Fat Free Cream Cheese
    with Garlic & Herbs
½ cup 2% low fat milk
¼ cup fat free sour cream
2 tablespoons fresh lemon juice
1 tablespoon prepared horseradish
½ teaspoon freshly ground black pepper
  Radish slices (optional)

1. In a food processor or blender, process all of the ingredients for 30 seconds or until well blended. Refrigerate until ready to serve. Garnish with the radish slices, if you wish.

2. Serve this dressing over vegetable or meat salads. It's also a great sauce for grilled meat, chicken and fish.

Makes 2 cups

NUTRIENTS PER SERVING			
Calories	34	Fat	0 g
Cholesterol	4 mg	Sodium	123 mg

Creamy Garlic Dressing

Vegetables & Side Dishes

• • • • • • • • • •

Country Green Beans with Ham

2   teaspoons olive oil
¼   cup minced onion
1   clove garlic, minced
1   pound fresh green beans, rinsed and drained
1   cup chopped fresh tomatoes
6   slices (2 ounces) thinly sliced low-fat smoked turkey-ham
1   tablespoon chopped fresh marjoram
2   teaspoons chopped fresh basil
⅛   teaspoon ground black pepper
¼   cup herbed croutons

1. Heat oil in medium saucepan over medium heat. Add onion and garlic; cook and stir about 3 minutes or until onion is tender. Reduce heat to low.

2. Add green beans, tomatoes, turkey-ham, marjoram, basil and black pepper. Cook about 10 minutes, stirring occasionally, until liquid from tomatoes is absorbed. Top with croutons.   *Makes 4 servings*

NUTRIENTS PER SERVING			
Calories	100	Fat	3 g
Cholesterol	12 mg	Sodium	194 mg

Country Green Beans with Ham

Mini Vegetable Quiches

2 cups cut-up vegetables (bell peppers, broccoli, zucchini
   and/or carrots)
2 tablespoons chopped green onions
2 tablespoons FLEISCHMANN'S® Margarine
4 (8-inch) flour tortillas, each cut into 8 triangles
1 cup EGG BEATERS® Healthy Real Egg Product
1 cup skim milk
½ teaspoon dried basil leaves

In medium nonstick skillet, over medium-high heat, sauté vegetables and green onions in margarine until tender.

Arrange 4 tortilla pieces in each of 8 (6-ounce) greased custard cups or ramekins, placing points of tortilla pieces at center of bottom of cup and pressing lightly to form shape of cup. Divide vegetable mixture evenly among cups. In small bowl, combine Egg Beaters®, milk and basil. Pour evenly over vegetable mixture. Place cups on baking sheet. Bake at 375°F for 20 to 25 minutes or until puffed and knife inserted into centers comes out clean. Let stand 5 minutes before serving.

Makes 8 servings

NUTRIENTS PER SERVING			
Calories	122	Fat	4 g
Cholesterol	1 mg	Sodium	198 mg

Stacked Burrito Pie

½ cup GUILTLESS GOURMET® Mild Black Bean Dip
2 teaspoons water
5 low fat flour tortillas (6 inches each)
½ cup nonfat sour cream or plain yogurt
½ cup GUILTLESS GOURMET® Roasted Red Pepper Salsa
1¼ cups (5 ounces) shredded low fat Monterey Jack cheese
4 cups shredded iceberg or romaine lettuce
½ cup GUILTLESS GOURMET® Salsa (mild, medium or hot)
Lime slices and chili pepper (optional)

Preheat oven to 350°F. Combine bean dip and 2 teaspoons water in small bowl; mix well. Line 7½-inch springform pan with 1 tortilla. Spread 2 tablespoons bean dip mixture over tortilla, then spread with 2 tablespoons sour cream and 2 tablespoons red pepper salsa. Sprinkle with ¼ cup cheese. Repeat layers 3 more times. Place remaining tortilla on top and sprinkle with remaining ¼ cup cheese.

Bake 40 minutes or until heated through. (Place sheet of foil under springform pan to catch any juices that may seep through the bottom.) Cool slightly before unmolding. To serve, cut into 4 quarters. Place 1 cup lettuce on 4 serving plates. Top each serving with 1 quarter burrito pie and 2 tablespoons salsa. Garnish with lime slices and pepper, if desired. *Makes 4 servings*

NUTRIENTS PER SERVING			
(1 quarter)			
Calories	302	Fat	7 g
Cholesterol	12 mg	Sodium	650 mg

Stacked Burrito Pie

256

Polenta with Black Bean Salsa

Olive oil-flavored nonstick cooking spray
2 teaspoons chicken flavor bouillon granules
¾ cup uncooked polenta or stone ground cornmeal
1 cup rinsed, drained canned black beans
¾ cup chunky salsa
⅔ cup frozen whole kernel corn, thawed
⅓ cup minced fresh cilantro
4 teaspoons olive oil
6 tablespoons nonfat sour cream (optional)

1. Spray 9-inch-square pan with cooking spray; set aside.

2. Combine 3 cups water and bouillon granules in large saucepan; bring to a boil over high heat. Gradually add polenta, stirring constantly with wire whisk. Reduce heat to medium-low. Simmer 10 to 15 minutes or until polenta is thickened and pulls away from side of pan, stirring constantly with wooden spoon. Spread polenta evenly into prepared pan. Cover with plastic wrap; refrigerate 1 to 2 hours or until polenta is firm.

3. Combine beans, salsa, corn and cilantro in medium bowl. Cover with plastic wrap; refrigerate 1 hour. Bring to room temperature before serving.

4. Cut polenta into 6 rectangles; cut each rectangle diagonally to form 2 triangles. Brush both sides of triangles with oil. Spray large nonstick skillet with cooking spray; heat over medium-high heat until hot. Cook triangles, 4 at a time, 6 to 8 minutes or until browned, turning once. Place 2 polenta triangles on each serving plate; top each serving evenly with black bean salsa and sour cream if desired. Garnish as desired. *Makes 6 servings*

NUTRIENTS PER SERVING			
Calories	136	Fat	4 g
Cholesterol	1 mg	Sodium	639 mg

Polenta with Black Bean Salsa

Vegetables in Garlic-Cream Sauce

1 cup water
4 cups cut-up vegetables such as DOLE® Asparagus, Bell
    Peppers, Broccoli, Carrots, Cauliflower or Sugar Peas
1 teaspoon olive or vegetable oil
4 garlic cloves, finely chopped
⅓ cup fat free or reduced fat mayonnaise
⅓ cup nonfat or low fat milk
2 tablespoons chopped fresh parsley

• **Place** water in large saucepan; bring to boil. Add vegetables; reduce heat to low. Cook, uncovered, 9 to 12 minutes or until vegetables are tender-crisp; meanwhile, prepare sauce.

• **Heat** oil in small saucepan over medium heat. Add garlic; cook and stir garlic until golden brown. Remove from heat; stir in mayonnaise and milk.

• **Drain** vegetables; place in serving bowl. Pour in garlic sauce; toss to evenly coat. Sprinkle with parsley. *Makes 4 servings*

Prep time: 10 minutes
Cook time: 15 minutes

NUTRIENTS PER SERVING			
Calories	89	Fat	2 g
Cholesterol	1 mg	Sodium	293 mg

New England Style Vegetables with Garlic-Cream Sauce: Substitute 2 packages (9 ounces each) DOLE® New England Style Vegetables for 4 cups cut-up vegetables. Cut potatoes in half. Cook vegetables according to package directions; drain. Place vegetables in serving bowl. Prepare sauce as directed above. Pour sauce over vegetables in serving bowl; toss to evenly coat. Sprinkle with parsley.

Indian-Style Vegetable Stir-Fry

1   teaspoon canola oil
1   teaspoon curry powder
1   teaspoon ground cumin
⅛   teaspoon red pepper flakes
1½ teaspoons finely chopped, seeded jalapeño pepper
2   cloves garlic, minced
¾   cup chopped red bell pepper
¾   cup thinly sliced carrots
3   cups cauliflower florets
½   cup water, divided
½   teaspoon salt
2   teaspoons finely chopped cilantro (optional)

1. Heat oil in large nonstick skillet over medium-high heat. Add curry powder, cumin and red pepper flakes; cook and stir about 30 seconds.

2. Stir in jalapeño and garlic. Add bell pepper and carrots; mix well to coat with spices. Add cauliflower; reduce heat to medium.

3. Stir in ¼ cup water; cook and stir until water evaporates. Add remaining ¼ cup water; cover and cook about 8 to 10 minutes or until vegetables are crisp-tender, stirring occasionally.

4. Add salt; mix well. Sprinkle with cilantro and garnish with mizuna and additional red bell pepper, if desired. Serve immediately.   *Makes 6 servings*

NUTRIENTS PER SERVING			
Calories	40	Fat	1 g
Cholesterol	0 mg	Sodium	198 mg

Vegetable Strata

2 slices white bread, cubed
¼ cup shredded reduced-fat Swiss cheese
½ cup sliced carrots
½ cup sliced mushrooms
¼ cup chopped onion
1 clove garlic, crushed
1 teaspoon FLEISCHMANN'S® Margarine
½ cup chopped tomato
½ cup snow peas
1 cup EGG BEATERS® Healthy Real Egg Product
¾ cup skim milk

Place bread cubes evenly into bottom of greased 1½-quart casserole dish. Sprinkle with cheese; set aside.

In medium nonstick skillet, over medium heat, sauté carrots, mushrooms, onion and garlic in margarine until tender. Stir in tomato and snow peas; cook 1 to 2 minutes more. Spoon over cheese. In small bowl, combine Egg Beaters® and milk; pour over vegetable mixture. Bake at 375°F for 45 to 50 minutes or until knife inserted in center comes out clean. Let stand 10 minutes before serving. *Makes 6 servings*

Prep time: 15 minutes
Cook time: 55 minutes

NUTRIENTS PER SERVING			
Calories	94	Fat	2 g
Cholesterol	3 mg	Sodium	161 mg

Vegetable Strata

Southwestern Twice-Baked Spuds

2   baking potatoes with skins (about 6 ounces each)
½   cup GUILTLESS GOURMET® Nacho Dip (mild or spicy)
¼   cup finely chopped green onions
¼   teaspoon coarsely ground black pepper
2   tablespoons GUILTLESS GOURMET® Salsa (mild, medium
      or hot)
2   tablespoons chopped fresh cilantro
     Nasturtium flowers (optional)

Preheat oven to 400°F. Scrub potatoes with vegetable brush; pierce in several places with fork. Bake potatoes 45 to 50 minutes or until fork-tender. Remove from oven; cool potatoes until safe enough to handle.

Reduce oven temperature to 300°F. Slice potatoes in half lengthwise. Form 4 shells by scooping out most of potato pulp, being careful not to pierce skin. Place pulp in large bowl; mash with potato masher or whip with electric mixer. Add nacho dip, onions and pepper. Blend until smooth. Add salsa and cilantro; mix until blended. Fill potato shells with equal amount of potato mixture, heaping to form mounds. Wrap skins in foil, leaving tops open. Place on baking sheet.

Bake 25 minutes or until heated through. Serve hot. Garnish with edible flowers, if desired.   *Makes 4 servings*

NUTRIENTS PER SERVING			
Calories	112	Fat	<1 g
Cholesterol	0 mg	Sodium	193 mg

Southwestern Twice-Baked Spud

South-of-the-Border Pizza

1 prepared pizza shell or crust (about 12 inches)
1 cup cooked low-sodium kidney beans, rinsed and drained
1 cup frozen whole kernel corn, thawed
1 tomato, chopped
¼ cup finely chopped fresh cilantro
1 jalapeño pepper, finely chopped
¼ cup (4 ounces) shredded reduced-fat Monterey Jack cheese

1. Preheat oven to 450°F. Place pizza shell on ungreased pizza pan or baking sheet.

2. Arrange beans, corn, tomato, cilantro and jalapeño over pizza shell. Sprinkle evenly with cheese.

3. Bake pizza 8 to 10 minutes or until cheese is melted and lightly browned. Garnish with green bell pepper, if desired.   *Makes 4 servings*

NUTRIENTS PER SERVING			
Calories	361	Fat	7 g
Cholesterol	20 mg	Sodium	569 mg

South-of-the-Border Pizza

Iowa Corn Pudding

½ cup egg substitute or 2 large eggs
2 large egg whites
3 tablespoons all-purpose flour
1 tablespoon sugar
½ teaspoon freshly ground black pepper
1 can (16½ ounces) cream-style corn
2 cups fresh corn kernels or frozen corn, thawed and drained
1 cup (4 ounces) shredded ALPINE LACE® American Flavor
   Pasteurized Process Cheese Product
½ cup finely chopped red bell pepper
⅓ cup 2% low fat milk
1 tablespoon unsalted butter substitute
¼ teaspoon paprika
   Sprigs of fresh parsley

268

1. Preheat the oven to 350°F. Spray an 8-inch round baking dish with nonstick cooking spray. (A deep-dish pie plate works well.) Place in the oven to heat.

2. Meanwhile, in a large bowl, using an electric mixer set on high, beat the egg substitute (or the whole eggs) and egg whites with the flour, sugar and black pepper until smooth. Stir in the creamed corn, corn kernels, cheese, bell pepper and milk. Pour into the hot baking dish.

3. Dot with the butter and sprinkle with the paprika. Bake, uncovered, for 55 minutes or until set. Let stand for 15 minutes before serving. Garnish with the parsley.   *Makes 6 servings*

NUTRIENTS PER SERVING			
Calories	226	Fat	6 g
Cholesterol	17 mg	Sodium	556 mg

Iowa Corn Pudding

Apple-Potato Pancakes

1¼ cups unpeeled, finely chopped apples
1 cup peeled, grated potatoes
½ cup MOTT'S® Natural Apple Sauce
½ cup all-purpose flour
2 egg whites
1 teaspoon salt
Additional MOTT'S® Natural Apple Sauce or apple slices
(optional)

1. Preheat oven to 475°F. Spray cookie sheet with nonstick cooking spray.

2. In medium bowl, combine apples, potatoes, ½ cup apple sauce, flour, egg whites and salt.

3. Spray large nonstick skillet with nonstick cooking spray; heat over medium heat until hot. Drop rounded tablespoonfuls of batter 2 inches apart into skillet. Cook 2 to 3 minutes on each side or until lightly browned. Place pancakes on prepared cookie sheet.

4. Bake 10 to 15 minutes or until crisp. Serve with additional apple sauce or apple slices, if desired. Refrigerate leftovers. *Makes 12 servings*

NUTRIENTS PER SERVING			
(1 pancake)			
Calories	60	Fat	0 g
Cholesterol	0 mg	Sodium	190 mg

Apple-Potato Pancakes

Garden-Style Risotto

1 can (14½ ounces) low-sodium chicken broth
1¾ cups water
2 garlic cloves, finely chopped
1 teaspoon dried basil leaves, crushed
½ teaspoon dried thyme leaves, crushed
1 cup arborio rice
2 cups packed DOLE® Fresh Spinach, torn
1 cup DOLE® Shredded Carrots
3 tablespoons grated Parmesan cheese

• **Combine** broth, water, garlic, basil and thyme in large saucepan. Bring to boil; meanwhile, prepare rice.

• **Place** rice in large, nonstick saucepan sprayed with vegetable cooking spray. Cook and stir rice over medium heat about 2 minutes or until rice is browned.

• **Pour** 1 cup boiling broth into saucepan with rice; cook, stirring constantly, until broth is almost absorbed (there should be some broth left).

• **Add** enough broth to barely cover rice; continue to cook, stirring constantly, until broth is almost absorbed. Repeat adding broth and cooking, stirring constantly, until broth is almost absorbed, about 15 minutes; add spinach and carrots with the last addition of broth.

• **Cook** 3 to 5 minutes more, stirring constantly, or until broth is almost absorbed and rice and vegetables are tender. *Do not overcook.* (Risotto will be saucy and have a creamy texture.) Stir in Parmesan cheese. Serve warm.

Makes 6 servings

Prep time: 5 minutes
Cook time: 25 minutes

continued on page 274

Garden-Style Risotto

Garden-Style Risotto, continued

Garden Pilaf: Substitute 1 cup uncooked long grain white rice for arborio rice and reduce water from 1¾ cups to ½ cup. Prepare broth as directed above with ½ cup water; meanwhile, brown rice as directed above. Carefully add browned rice into boiling broth. Reduce heat to low; cover and cook 15 minutes. Stir in vegetables; cover and cook 4 to 5 minutes longer or until rice and vegetables are tender. Stir in Parmesan cheese.

NUTRIENTS PER SERVING			
Calories	170	Fat	2 g
Cholesterol	4 mg	Sodium	155 mg

Fruity Wild Rice Side Dish

¼ cup margarine
½ cup walnuts, coarsely chopped
½ cup diced dried fruit bits
3 cups cooked wild rice
¼ cup packed brown sugar
   Ground cinnamon

In skillet, melt margarine. Add walnuts and dried fruit; cook over low heat 5 minutes. Blend into wild rice. Sprinkle with brown sugar and cinnamon.

Makes 6 servings

NUTRIENTS PER SERVING			
Calories	185	Fat	8 g
Cholesterol	0 mg	Sodium	42 mg

Favorite recipe from **Minnesota Cultivated Wild Rice Council**

274

Risotto with Vegetables

1½ tablespoons margarine
1½ tablespoons olive oil
1 cup sliced mushrooms
½ cup chopped onion
1 clove garlic, minced
1 cup uncooked arborio rice
Pinch saffron (optional)
2 cups hot low-sodium chicken broth, divided
½ teaspoon TABASCO® pepper sauce
1 to 1½ cups hot water, divided
1 package (9 ounces) frozen artichoke hearts, cooked and
drained
½ cup coarsely chopped roasted red peppers*

In large skillet heat margarine and oil over medium heat. Add mushrooms, onion and garlic; cook 5 minutes or until onion is translucent. Stir in rice; cook 1 to 2 minutes or until partly translucent. Add saffron, if desired. Add ½ cup hot broth and TABASCO pepper sauce; stir constantly until rice absorbs broth. Add remaining broth and hot water, ½ cup at a time, stirring constantly from bottom and side of pan. (Wait until rice just begins to dry out before adding more liquid.) Cook and stir until rice is tender but firm to the bite and the risotto is the consistency of creamy rice pudding. (The total amount of liquid used will vary. Watch rice carefully to ensure proper consistency.) Total cooking time is about 30 minutes. Stir in artichokes and roasted peppers. Serve with additional TABASCO pepper sauce, if desired. *Makes 6 servings*

*To roast peppers, hold over source of heat with a fork until skin blisters. Cool slightly; peel and chop.

NUTRIENTS PER SERVING			
Calories	211	Fat	7 g
Cholesterol	0 mg	Sodium	59 mg

Athenian Rice with Feta Cheese

1   tablespoon olive oil
1   cup chopped red onion
1   red bell pepper, chopped
1   clove garlic, minced
3   cups cooked rice
½   cup sun-dried tomatoes, softened* and cut into julienne
       strips
1   can (4½ ounces) sliced black olives
1   tablespoon chopped fresh parsley
1½   teaspoons dried oregano leaves
½   cup crumbled feta cheese
1   tablespoon lemon juice
¼   teaspoon ground black pepper
       Fresh oregano for garnish

Heat oil in large skillet over medium-high heat until hot. Add onion, red pepper and garlic; cook and stir until onion is tender. Stir in rice, tomatoes, olives, parsley and oregano; heat thoroughly. Remove from heat; add cheese, lemon juice and black pepper. Stir until well blended. Garnish with oregano. Serve immediately.   *Makes 6 servings*

*To soften sun-dried tomatoes, place in ⅓ cup boiling water; stir to coat. Let stand 10 minutes; drain water.

NUTRIENTS PER SERVING			
Calories	204	Fat	7 g
Cholesterol	8 mg	Sodium	612 mg

Favorite recipe from **USA Rice Council**

Athenian Rice with Feta Cheese

Couscous with Chick-peas and Vegetables

1 cup dried chick-peas (garbanzo beans)
2 cans (14 ounces each) fat-free reduced-sodium chicken broth
1 large onion, quartered and sliced
2 large cloves garlic, minced
1 teaspoon ground cinnamon
1 teaspoon red pepper flakes
½ teaspoon paprika
½ teaspoon saffron or turmeric (optional)
½ teaspoon salt
½ pound eggplant, cut into ¾-inch cubes
1 large sweet potato, peeled and cut into ¾-inch cubes
¾ pound zucchini, cut into ¾-inch cubes
1 can (14½ ounces) chopped tomatoes
2 tablespoons finely chopped fresh parsley
2 tablespoons finely chopped fresh cilantro
4 cups hot cooked couscous, cooked without salt

1. Sort and rinse chick-peas. Cover with water and let soak overnight; drain. Place in Dutch oven with chicken broth; bring to a boil over high heat.

2. Add onion, garlic, cinnamon, red pepper flakes, paprika and saffron; reduce heat to low. Cover and simmer 1 hour or until beans are tender. Stir in salt.

3. Add eggplant and sweet potato; cook 10 minutes. Add zucchini and tomatoes; cook 10 minutes or just until all vegetables are tender. Stir in parsley and cilantro; spoon mixture over hot couscous. Garnish with sweet potato slices and chives, if desired.

Makes 6 servings

NUTRIENTS PER SERVING			
Calories	324	Fat	2 g
Cholesterol	0 mg	Sodium	330 mg

Couscous with Chick-peas and Vegetables

Alpine Fettuccine

½ pound white fettuccine, preferably fresh
½ pound green fettuccine, preferably fresh
1½ teaspoons extra virgin olive oil
1 cup sliced fresh mushrooms
1 cup chopped red bell pepper
½ cup skim milk
6 ounces (1 carton) ALPINE LACE® Fat Free Cream Cheese
with Garlic & Herbs

1. Cook the fettuccine according to package directions until al dente. Drain well and place in a large shallow pasta bowl. Toss with the oil and keep warm.

2. Meanwhile, spray a medium-size nonstick skillet with nonstick cooking spray. Add the mushrooms and bell pepper and sauté until soft. Toss with the fettuccine.

3. In a small saucepan, bring the milk to a boil over medium heat. Add the cream cheese and stir until melted. Toss with pasta and serve immediately.

Makes 9 side-dish servings (1 cup each) or
6 main-dish servings (1½ cups each)

NUTRIENTS PER SERVING			
Calories	228	Fat	3 g
Cholesterol	51 mg	Sodium	138 mg

Alpine Fettuccine

Fresh Vegetable Lasagna

8 ounces uncooked lasagna noodles
1 package (10 ounces) frozen chopped spinach, thawed and
  well drained
1 cup shredded carrots
½ cup sliced green onions
½ cup sliced red bell pepper
¼ cup chopped fresh parsley
½ teaspoon ground black pepper
1½ cups low-fat cottage cheese
1 cup buttermilk
½ cup plain nonfat yogurt
2 egg whites
1 cup sliced mushrooms
1 can (14 ounces) artichoke hearts, drained and chopped
2 cups (8 ounces) shredded part-skim mozzarella cheese
¼ cup freshly grated Parmesan cheese

1. Cook pasta according to package directions, omitting salt. Drain. Rinse under cold water; drain well. Set aside.

2. Preheat oven to 375°F. Pat spinach with paper towels to remove excess moisture. Combine spinach, carrots, green onions, bell pepper, parsley and black pepper in large bowl. Set aside.

3. Combine cottage cheese, buttermilk, yogurt and egg whites in food processor or blender; process until smooth.

4. Spray 13×9-inch baking pan with nonstick cooking spray. Arrange half of lasagna noodles in bottom of pan. Spread with half each of cottage cheese mixture, vegetable mixture, mushrooms, artichokes and mozzarella. Repeat layers, ending with noodles. Sprinkle with Parmesan.

continued on page 284

Fresh Vegetable Lasagna

Fresh Vegetable Lasagna, continued

5. Cover and bake 30 minutes. Remove cover; continue baking 20 minutes or until bubbly and heated through. Let stand 10 minutes before serving.

Makes 8 servings

NUTRIENTS PER SERVING			
Calories	250	Fat	8 g
Cholesterol	22 mg	Sodium	508 mg

Pineapple Noodle Pudding

1¼ cups cooked macaroni
1 cup unsweetened canned pineapple chunks, juice reserved
¾ cup low-fat cottage cheese
¼ cup imitation sour cream
1 egg white
3 tablespoons dark brown sugar
¼ cup wheat flakes
1 tablespoon granulated sugar
¼ teaspoon cinnamon

Preheat oven to 350°F. Spray 1-quart casserole dish with nonstick cooking spray. Measure ¼ cup juice from pineapple; discard any remaining juice. In large bowl combine macaroni, pineapple, ¼ cup reserved juice, cottage cheese, sour cream, egg white and brown sugar. Pour into casserole dish. In small bowl mix wheat flakes, granulated sugar and cinnamon. Sprinkle flake topping over noodle mixture. Bake uncovered 25 minutes or until bubbly. *Makes 6 servings*

NUTRIENTS PER SERVING			
Calories	138	Fat	2 g
Cholesterol	1 mg	Sodium	149 mg

Favorite recipe from **The Sugar Association, Inc.**

Creamy Macaroni and Cheese

2 tablespoons CRISCO® Oil
½ cup chopped green onions with tops
1 clove garlic, minced
2 tablespoons all-purpose flour
¼ teaspoon dried basil leaves
¼ teaspoon dry mustard
⅛ teaspoon pepper
2 cups skim milk
1 cup (4 ounces) shredded (⅓ less fat) sharp Cheddar cheese
½ cup nonfat sour cream alternative
1 teaspoon Worcestershire sauce
  Dash of hot pepper sauce
1½ cups uncooked small elbow macaroni, cooked (without salt or
    fat) and well drained
1 tablespoon plain dry bread crumbs

1. Heat oven to 350°F. Oil 2-quart casserole lightly. Set aside.

2. Heat 2 tablespoons oil in large skillet on medium heat. Add onions and garlic. Cook and stir until tender.

3. Stir in flour, basil, dry mustard and pepper. Stir until well blended. Stir in milk. Cook and stir until mixture thickens and just comes to a boil. Stir in cheese, "sour cream," Worcestershire sauce and hot pepper sauce.

4. Combine macaroni and sauce in large bowl. Toss to coat. Spoon into casserole. Sprinkle with bread crumbs.

5. Bake at 350°F for 25 minutes. *Makes 6 servings*

NUTRIENTS PER SERVING			
Calories	260	Fat	9 g
Cholesterol	15 mg	Sodium	215 mg

Stuffed Shells Florentine

1 cup (about 4 ounces) coarsely chopped mushrooms
½ cup chopped onion
1 clove garlic, minced
1 teaspoon Italian seasoning
¼ teaspoon ground black pepper
1 tablespoon FLEISCHMANN'S® Margarine
1 (16-ounce) container fat-free cottage cheese
1 (10-ounce) package frozen chopped spinach, thawed and well
    drained
½ cup EGG BEATERS® Healthy Real Egg Product
24 jumbo pasta shells, cooked in unsalted water and drained
1 (15¼-ounce) jar reduced-sodium spaghetti sauce

In large skillet, over medium-high heat, sauté mushrooms, onion, garlic, Italian seasoning and pepper in margarine until tender. Remove from heat; stir in cottage cheese, spinach and Egg Beaters®. Spoon mixture into shells.

Spread ½ cup spaghetti sauce in bottom of 13×9×2-inch baking dish; arrange shells over sauce. Top with remaining sauce; cover. Bake at 350°F for 35 minutes or until hot.   *Makes 7 servings*

Prep time: 30 minutes
Cook time: 40 minutes

NUTRIENTS PER SERVING			
Calories	255	Fat	2 g
Cholesterol	6 mg	Sodium	515 mg

Cakes & Cheesecakes

• • • • • • • • • •

Black Forest Chocolate Fudge Cake

2	cups cake flour
1	cup unsweetened cocoa powder
1	teaspoon baking powder
½	teaspoon salt
1½	cups packed brown sugar
2	eggs
1	egg white
1	cup Prune Purée (page 90) or prepared prune butter
¾	cup nonfat milk
4	teaspoons vanilla
1	cup boiling water
2	tablespoons instant espresso coffee powder
2	teaspoons baking soda
2	cups frozen pitted unsweetened dark sweet cherries, coarsely chopped, thawed and well drained
½	cup chopped toasted walnuts
	Mocha Glaze (page 290)
	Chocolate Drizzle (optional, page 290)
	Fresh cherries or frozen cherries, thawed
	Mint sprigs, for garnish

continued on page 290

Black Forest Chocolate Fudge Cake

Black Forest Chocolate Fudge Cake, continued

Preheat oven to 350°F. Coat 12- to 16-cup Bundt or other tube pan with vegetable cooking spray. In large bowl, combine flour, cocoa, baking powder and salt; mix in brown sugar. In medium bowl, whisk eggs, egg white, Prune Purée, milk and vanilla. In 2-cup measure, combine boiling water, espresso powder and baking soda. Stir prune and water mixtures into flour mixture; mix just until blended. Pour half the batter into prepared pan; sprinkle cherries and walnuts evenly over batter. Top with remaining batter. Bake in center of oven about 45 minutes until pick inserted into center comes out clean. Cool in pan on wire rack 15 minutes; remove from pan. Cool completely on wire rack. Prepare Mocha Glaze. Spoon over cake, allowing glaze to run down sides. Prepare Chocolate Drizzle, if desired. Drizzle over glaze. Fill cake center with additional cherries and garnish with mint.   *Makes 16 servings*

Mocha Glaze: Place 1 cup powdered sugar in small bowl. Dissolve ⅛ teaspoon instant espresso coffee powder in 4 teaspoons water. Stir into sugar until smooth, adding 1 teaspoon water, if needed, for desired consistency.

Chocolate Drizzle: In top of double boiler or bowl set over simmering water, melt 2 tablespoons semisweet chocolate chips. Stir in 2 teaspoons hot water until blended. Cool until desired consistency.

NUTRIENTS PER SERVING			
Calories	221	Fat	4 g
Cholesterol	27 mg	Sodium	201 mg

Favorite recipe from **California Prune Board**

Trimtime Chocolate Cake Roll

½ cup all-purpose flour
¼ cup HERSHEY®S European Style Cocoa or HERSHEY®S Cocoa
1 teaspoon baking powder
4 eggs
⅓ cup sugar
1 teaspoon vanilla extract
2 cups (1 pint) vanilla nonfat frozen yogurt, slightly softened
  Powdered sugar (optional)

1. Heat oven to 400°F. Spray 15½×10½×1-inch jelly-roll pan with vegetable cooking spray. Line with waxed paper; spray again.

2. Sift together flour, cocoa and baking powder. In small mixer bowl, beat eggs, sugar and vanilla until pale in color, about 5 minutes. Fold in cocoa mixture; spread batter into prepared pan.

3. Bake 5 to 7 minutes or until top springs back when touched lightly in center. Invert cake onto clean towel; remove waxed paper. Roll up cake with towel from short side. Cool completely on wire rack.

4. Unroll cake; spread with frozen yogurt. Reroll cake without towel; press seam side down. Cover; freeze until firm. Sprinkle top lightly with powdered sugar, if desired. Cover; freeze leftover cake roll. *Makes 12 servings*

NUTRIENTS PER SERVING			
Calories	130	Fat	2 g
Cholesterol	70 mg	Sodium	95 mg

Mocha Marble Pound Cake

2 cups all-purpose flour
2 teaspoons DAVIS® Baking Powder
1 teaspoon baking soda
½ teaspoon salt
1 cup sugar
¼ cup FLEISCHMANN'S® Margarine, softened
1 teaspoon vanilla extract
½ cup EGG BEATERS® Healthy Real Egg Product
1 (8-ounce) container low fat coffee yogurt
¼ cup unsweetened cocoa
   Mocha Yogurt Glaze (recipe follows)

In small bowl, combine flour, baking powder, baking soda and salt; set aside. In large bowl, with electric mixer at medium speed, beat sugar, margarine and vanilla until creamy. Add Egg Beaters®; beat until smooth. With mixer at low speed, add yogurt alternately with flour mixture, beating well after each addition. Remove half of batter to medium bowl. Beat cocoa into batter remaining in large bowl. Alternately spoon coffee and chocolate batters into greased 9×5×3-inch loaf pan. Cut through batters for marbled effect. Bake at 325°F for 60 to 65 minutes or until toothpick inserted in center comes out clean. Cool in pan on wire rack 10 minutes. Remove from pan; cool completely on wire rack. Frost with Mocha Yogurt Glaze. *Makes 16 servings*

Mocha Yogurt Glaze: In small bowl, combine ½ cup powdered sugar, 1 tablespoon unsweetened cocoa and 1 tablespoon low fat coffee yogurt until smooth; add more yogurt if necessary to make spreading consistency.

Prep time: 20 minutes
Cook time: 65 minutes

NUTRIENTS PER SERVING			
Calories	159	Fat	3 g
Sodium	215 mg	Cholesterol	1 mg

Mocha Marble Pound Cake

A Lighter Chocolate Decadence

1¼ cups sugar, divided
⅔ cup unsweetened cocoa powder
2 tablespoons all-purpose flour
¾ cup nonfat milk
5 ounces semisweet chocolate chips (about ¾ cup)
¼ cup Prune Purée (page 90) or prepared prune butter
1 egg
1 egg yolk
1 teaspoon vanilla
2 egg whites
⅛ teaspoon cream of tartar
    Raspberry Sauce (page 296)
1½ cups low fat nondairy whipped topping
    Fresh raspberries and mint leaves, for garnish

Preheat oven to 350°F. Line 9-inch round layer cake pan with parchment paper or waxed paper; coat with vegetable cooking spray. In medium saucepan, combine 1 cup sugar, cocoa and flour. Slowly whisk in milk until blended. Bring to a simmer over low heat, stirring constantly. Place chocolate chips in large bowl; pour in hot mixture, stirring until chocolate melts. Whisk in Prune Purée, egg, egg yolk and vanilla until blended. Set aside to cool. In mixer bowl, beat egg whites with cream of tartar until foamy. Gradually beat in remaining ¼ cup sugar until stiff peaks form. Fold half the egg white mixture into cooled chocolate mixture; fold in remaining egg white mixture. Pour into prepared pan. Bake in center of oven 30 to 35 minutes until puffy and center is set but still moist. (Do not overbake.) Cool completely in pan on wire rack. (Cake will sink as it cools.) Remove from pan. Wrap securely; chill 24 hours before serving. Prepare Raspberry Sauce. Cut dessert into wedges; serve with Raspberry Sauce and whipped topping. Garnish with raspberries and mint leaves.

Makes 12 servings

continued on page 296

A Lighter Chocolate Decadence

294

A Lighter Chocolate Decadence, continued

Raspberry Sauce: Puree 1 package (12 ounces) thawed frozen raspberries in blender; strain. Sweeten to taste with sugar. Makes 1 cup.

NUTRIENTS PER SERVING			
Calories	200	Fat	10 g
Cholesterol	35 mg	Sodium	30 mg

Favorite recipe from **California Prune Board**

Sensibly Delicious Chocolate Chip Snacking Cake

- 2 cups all-purpose flour
- ¾ cup granulated sugar
- 1 teaspoon baking soda
- ½ teaspoon ground cinnamon
- ¼ teaspoon salt
- ¾ cup unsweetened applesauce
- ¼ cup nonfat milk
- ¼ cup margarine, melted
- 1 egg white
- 2 teaspoons vanilla extract
- 2 cups (12-ounce package) NESTLÉ® TOLL HOUSE® Semi-Sweet Chocolate Morsels, divided

COMBINE flour, sugar, baking soda, cinnamon and salt in large bowl. Stir in applesauce, milk, margarine, egg white and vanilla just until blended. Stir in *1 cup* morsels. Spoon into greased 9×9-inch baking pan. Sprinkle with *remaining* morsels.

BAKE in preheated 350°F oven for 25 to 35 minutes or until wooden pick inserted in center comes out clean. Cool in pan. Cut into 2¼-inch squares.

Makes 16 servings

NUTRIENTS PER SERVING			
Calories	240	Fat	10 g
Cholesterol	0 mg	Sodium	150 mg

Sensibly Delicious Chocolate Pound Cake

  3   cups all-purpose flour
 ⅓   cup NESTLÉ® TOLL HOUSE® Baking Cocoa
  1   tablespoon baking powder
 ½   teaspoon salt
  2   cups packed light brown sugar
 ½   cup LIBBY'S® Solid Pack Pumpkin
  6   tablespoons margarine
  4   teaspoons vanilla extract
  5   egg whites, at room temperature
  2   cups (12-ounce package) NESTLÉ® TOLL HOUSE®
        Semi-Sweet Chocolate Morsels
1⅔   cups nonfat milk
        Powdered sugar and fresh berries (optional)

COMBINE flour, cocoa, baking powder and salt in medium bowl. Beat brown sugar, pumpkin, margarine and vanilla in large mixer bowl. Add egg whites; beat on medium speed for 2 minutes.

MELT morsels in small, heavy saucepan over low heat, stirring until smooth; beat into creamed mixture. Gradually beat in flour mixture, alternating with milk. Spoon into 10-inch Bundt pan sprayed with no-stick cooking spray.

BAKE in preheated 350°F oven for 50 to 60 minutes or until wooden pick inserted near center comes out clean. Cool in pan for 30 minutes. Invert onto wire rack to cool completely. Sprinkle with powdered sugar; serve with berries.

Makes 24 servings

NUTRIENTS PER SERVING			
Calories	245	Fat	8 g
Cholesterol	0 mg	Sodium	165 mg

HERSHEY'S Slimmed Down Chocolate Cake

6   tablespoons (40% corn oil) lower-fat margarine
1   cup sugar
1   cup skim milk
1   tablespoon white vinegar
½   teaspoon vanilla extract
1¼ cups all-purpose flour
⅓   cup HERSHEY'S Cocoa
1   teaspoon baking soda
    Slimmed Down Cocoa Frosting (recipe follows)

Heat oven to 350°F. Spray two 8-inch round baking pans with vegetable cooking spray. In medium saucepan over low heat, melt margarine; stir in sugar. Remove from heat. Add milk, vinegar and vanilla; stir until blended. Stir together flour, cocoa and baking soda. Add to sugar mixture; stir until well blended. Pour batter evenly into prepared pans. Bake 20 minutes or until wooden pick inserted in centers comes out clean. Cool 10 minutes; remove from pans to wire racks. Cool completely. Prepare Slimmed Down Cocoa Frosting. Spread one cake layer with half of prepared frosting. Place second cake layer on top; spread remaining frosting over top of cake. Refrigerate 2 to 3 hours or until chilled. Garnish as desired. Cover; refrigerate leftover cake.

Makes 12 servings

SLIMMED DOWN COCOA FROSTING

1   envelope (1.3 ounces) dry whipped topping mix
1   tablespoon HERSHEY'S Cocoa
½   cup cold skim milk
½   teaspoon vanilla extract

In small, deep narrow-bottom mixer bowl, stir together topping mix and 1 tablespoon cocoa. Add ½ cup milk and ½ teaspoon vanilla. Beat on high speed of electric mixer about 4 minutes until soft peaks form.

continued on page 300

HERSHEY'S Slimmed Down Chocolate Cake

298

NUTRIENTS PER SERVING			
Calories	160	Fat	4 g
Cholesterol	0 mg	Sodium	120 mg

Chocolate Roulade with Creamy Yogurt Filling

Creamy Yogurt Filling (page 302)
3 egg whites
½ cup granulated sugar, divided
1 container (8 ounces) liquid egg substitute
½ cup cake flour
¼ cup HERSHEY®S Cocoa
1 teaspoon baking powder
⅛ teaspoon salt
2 tablespoons water
1 teaspoon vanilla extract
2 teaspoons powdered sugar
Peach Sauce (page 302)

Prepare Creamy Yogurt Filling. Heat oven to 375°F. Line 15½×10½×1-inch jelly-roll pan with foil; spray with vegetable cooking spray. In large mixer bowl, beat egg whites on high speed of electric mixer until foamy. Gradually add ¼ cup granulated sugar, beating well after each addition until stiff peaks hold their shape, sugar is dissolved and mixture is glossy. In small mixer bowl, beat egg substitute on medium speed until foamy; gradually add remaining ¼ cup granulated sugar, beating until mixture is thick. Fold egg substitute mixture into egg white mixture. In another small bowl, stir together flour, cocoa, baking powder and salt; gently fold into egg mixture alternately with water and vanilla. Spread batter evenly into prepared pan.

continued on page 302

Chocolate Roulade with Creamy Yogurt Filling

Chocolate Roulade with Creamy Yogurt Filling, continued

Bake 10 to 12 minutes or until top springs back when touched lightly in center. Immediately invert onto clean dishtowel sprinkled with powdered sugar; peel off foil. Roll up cake with towel from short side. Cool completely on wire rack. Unroll cake; remove towel. Spread with Creamy Yogurt Filling to within ½ inch of edges of cake. Reroll cake; place, seam-side down, on serving plate. Cover; refrigerate 2 to 3 hours or until chilled before serving. (Cake should be eaten same day as prepared.) Serve with Peach Sauce. Garnish as desired.

Makes 10 servings

CREAMY YOGURT FILLING

Yogurt Cheese (recipe follows)
1   envelope (1.3 ounces) dry whipped topping mix
⅓   cup cold skim milk
1   teaspoon vanilla extract
⅛   to ¼ teaspoon almond extract

Prepare Yogurt Cheese. Prepare topping mix as directed on package, using ⅓ cup milk, 1 teaspoon vanilla and almond extract. Gently fold Yogurt Cheese into whipped topping.

Yogurt Cheese: Use one 8-ounce container plain nonfat yogurt, no gelatin added. Line non-rusting colander or sieve with large piece of double thickness cheesecloth or large coffee filter; place colander over deep bowl. Spoon yogurt into prepared colander; cover with plastic wrap. Refrigerate until liquid no longer drains from yogurt, about 24 hours. Remove yogurt from cheesecloth and place in separate bowl; discard liquid.

Peach Sauce: In blender container, place 1½ cups fresh peach slices and 1 tablespoon sugar. Cover; blend until smooth. In medium microwave-safe bowl, stir together ¼ cup water and 1½ teaspoons cornstarch until dissolved. Add peach mixture; stir. Microwave at HIGH (100%) 2½ to 3 minutes or until mixture boils and thickens, stirring after each minute. Cool completely.

NUTRIENTS PER SERVING			
Calories	140	Fat	1 g
Cholesterol	0 mg	Sodium	130 mg

Four Way Fudgey Chocolate Cake

1¼ cups all-purpose flour
  1 cup sugar
  1 cup skim milk
  ⅓ cup HERSHEY®S Cocoa or HERSHEY®S European Style Cocoa
  ⅓ cup unsweetened applesauce
  1 tablespoon white vinegar
  1 teaspoon baking soda
  ½ teaspoon vanilla extract
    Toppings (optional): Frozen light non-dairy whipped topping,
      thawed, REESE®S Peanut Butter Chips, sliced strawberries,
      chopped almonds, raspberries

Heat oven to 350°F. Spray 9-inch square baking pan or 11×7×2-inch baking pan with vegetable cooking spray. In large mixer bowl, stir together flour, sugar, milk, cocoa, applesauce, vinegar, baking soda and vanilla; beat on low speed of electric mixer until blended. Pour batter into prepared pan. Bake 30 to 35 minutes or until wooden pick inserted in center comes out clean. Cool completely in pan on wire rack. If desired, spoon whipped topping into pastry bag fitted with star tip; pipe stars in two lines to divide cake into four squares or rectangles. Using plain tip, pipe lattice design into one square; place peanut butter chips onto lattice. Place strawberries into another square. Sprinkle almonds into third square. Place raspberries into remaining square. Serve immediately. Cover; refrigerate leftover cake. Store ungarnished cake, covered, at room temperature. *Makes 12 servings*

NUTRIENTS PER SERVING			
(no toppings)			
Calories	130	Fat	0 g
Cholesterol	0 mg	Sodium	80 mg

Pineapple Upside-Down Cake

1   (8-ounce) can crushed pineapple in juice, undrained
2   tablespoons margarine, melted, divided
½   cup firmly packed light brown sugar
6   whole maraschino cherries
1½ cups all-purpose flour
2   tablespoons baking powder
¼   teaspoon salt
1   cup granulated sugar
½   cup MOTT'S® Natural Apple Sauce
1   whole egg
3   egg whites, beaten until stiff

1. Preheat oven to 375°F. Drain pineapple; reserve juice. Spray sides of 8-inch square baking pan with nonstick cooking spray.

2. Spread 1 tablespoon melted margarine evenly in bottom of prepared pan. Sprinkle with brown sugar; top with pineapple. Slice cherries in half. Arrange cherries, cut side up, so that when cake is cut, each piece will have cherry half in center.

3. In small bowl, combine flour, baking powder and salt. In large bowl, combine granulated sugar, apple sauce, whole egg, remaining 1 tablespoon melted margarine and reserved pineapple juice.

4. Add flour mixture to apple sauce mixture; stir until well blended. Fold in beaten egg whites. Gently pour batter over fruit, spreading evenly.

5. Bake 35 to 40 minutes or until lightly browned. Cool on wire rack 10 minutes. Invert cake onto serving plate. Serve warm or cool completely. Cut into 12 pieces.

Makes 12 servings

NUTRIENTS PER SERVING			
Calories	200	Fat	3 g
Cholesterol	20 mg	Sodium	240 mg

Pineapple Upside-Down Cake

Polenta Apricot Pudding Cake

¼ cup chopped dried apricots
2 cups orange juice
1 cup part-skim ricotta cheese
3 tablespoons honey
¾ cup sugar
½ cup cornmeal
½ cup all-purpose flour
¼ teaspoon grated nutmeg
¼ cup slivered almonds

1. Preheat oven to 300°F. Soak apricots in ¼ cup water in small bowl 15 minutes. Drain and discard water. Pat apricots dry with paper towels; set aside.

2. Combine orange juice, ricotta cheese and honey in medium bowl. Mix on medium speed of electric mixer 5 minutes or until smooth. Combine sugar, cornmeal, flour and nutmeg in small bowl. Gradually add sugar mixture to orange juice mixture; blend well. Slowly stir in apricots.

3. Spray 10-inch nonstick springform pan with nonstick cooking spray. Pour batter into prepared pan. Sprinkle with almonds. Bake 60 to 70 minutes or until center is firm and cake is golden brown. Garnish with powdered sugar, if desired. Serve warm.   *Makes 8 servings*

NUTRIENTS PER SERVING			
Calories	245	Fat	5 g
Cholesterol	10 mg	Sodium	43 mg

Polenta Apricot Pudding Cake

Angel Food Cake with Pineapple Sauce

1   can (20 ounces) DOLE® Crushed Pineapple
1   tablespoon orange marmalade, peach or apricot fruit spread
2   tablespoons sugar
1   tablespoon cornstarch
1   prepared angel food cake

• **Combine** undrained pineapple, orange marmalade, sugar and cornstarch in small saucepan. Bring to boil. Reduce heat to low; cook 2 minutes, stirring constantly, or until sauce thickens. Cool slightly. Sauce can be served warm or chilled. Cut angel food cake into 12 slices. To serve, spoon sauce over each slice.

Makes 12 servings

NUTRIENTS PER SERVING			
Calories	116	Fat	0 g
Cholesterol	0 mg	Sodium	213 mg

Chocolate Swirled Cheesecake

Yogurt Cheese (page 310)
2   tablespoons graham cracker crumbs
1   package (8 ounces) Neufchâtel cheese (light cream cheese), softened
1½ teaspoons vanilla extract
¾   cup sugar
1   tablespoon cornstarch
1   container (8 ounces) liquid egg substitute
¼   cup HERSHEY®S Cocoa
¼   teaspoon almond extract

continued on page 310

Chocolate Swirled Cheesecake

Chocolate Swirled Cheesecake, continued

Prepare Yogurt Cheese. Heat oven to 325°F. Spray bottom of 8- or 9-inch springform pan with vegetable cooking spray. Sprinkle graham cracker crumbs on bottom of pan. In large mixer bowl, beat Yogurt Cheese, Neufchâtel cheese and vanilla on medium speed of electric mixer until smooth. Add sugar and cornstarch; beat just until well blended. Gradually add egg substitute, beating on low speed until blended. Transfer 1½ cups batter to medium bowl; add cocoa. Beat until well blended. Stir almond extract into vanilla batter. Alternately spoon vanilla and chocolate batters into prepared pan. With knife or metal spatula, cut through batters for marble effect.

Bake 35 minutes for 8-inch pan, 40 minutes for 9-inch pan or until edge is set. With knife, loosen cheesecake from side of pan. Cool completely in pan on wire rack. Cover; refrigerate at least 6 hours before serving. Just before serving, remove side of pan. Garnish as desired. Cover; refrigerate leftover cheesecake.

Makes 16 servings

Yogurt Cheese: Use one 16-ounce container plain lowfat yogurt, no gelatin added. Line colander with large piece of double thickness cheesecloth; place over deep bowl. Spoon yogurt into colander; cover with plastic wrap. Refrigerate until liquid no longer drains from yogurt, about 24 hours. Remove yogurt from cheesecloth; discard liquid.

NUTRIENTS PER SERVING			
Calories	100	Fat	4 g
Cholesterol	10 mg	Sodium	90 mg

310

Trimmed Down Chocoberry Cheesecake

Graham Crust (recipe follows)
1   cup (8 ounces) nonfat cottage cheese
1   package (8 ounces) Neufchâtel cheese (light cream cheese),
    softened
1   cup sugar
⅓   cup HERSHEY₂S Cocoa or HERSHEY₂S European Style Cocoa
1   package (10 ounces) frozen strawberries in syrup, thawed and
    drained
⅓   cup liquid egg substitute
    Frozen light non-dairy whipped topping, thawed (optional)
    Additional strawberries (optional)

Prepare Graham Crust. Heat oven to 325°F. In food processor, place cottage cheese; process until smooth. Add Neufchâtel cheese, sugar, cocoa and 1 package strawberries; process until smooth. Stir in egg substitute. Pour gently over prepared Graham Crust.

Bake 55 to 60 minutes or just until almost set in center. With knife, loosen cheesecake from side of pan. Cool completely in pan on wire rack. Cover; refrigerate until chilled. Just before serving, remove side of pan. Serve with whipped topping and additional strawberries, if desired. Cover; refrigerate leftover cheesecake. *Makes 14 servings*

Graham Crust: In small bowl, stir together ½ cup graham cracker crumbs and 1 tablespoon melted margarine; press onto bottom of 8-inch springform pan.

NUTRIENTS PER SERVING			
Calories	160	Fat	5 g
Cholesterol	15 mg	Sodium	150 mg

Luscious Chocolate Cheesecake

2 cups (1 pound) nonfat cottage cheese
¾ cup liquid egg substitute
⅔ cup sugar
4 ounces (½ of 8-ounce package) Neufchâtel cheese, softened
⅓ cup HERSHEY₃S Cocoa or HERSHEY₃S European Style Cocoa
½ teaspoon vanilla extract
  Yogurt Topping (recipe follows)
  Sliced strawberries, raspberries or mandarin orange
    segments (optional)

Heat oven to 300°F. Spray 9-inch springform pan with vegetable cooking spray. In food processor, place cottage cheese, egg substitute, sugar, Neufchâtel cheese, cocoa and vanilla; process until smooth. Pour into prepared pan. Bake 35 minutes or until edges are set. Meanwhile, prepare Yogurt Topping. Carefully spread topping over cheesecake. Continue baking 5 minutes. Remove from oven to wire rack. With knife, loosen cheesecake from side of pan. Cool completely. Cover; refrigerate until chilled. Remove side of pan. Serve with strawberries or mandarin orange segments, if desired. Refrigerate leftover cheesecake.

Makes 12 servings

YOGURT TOPPING

⅔ cup plain nonfat yogurt
2 tablespoons sugar

In small bowl, stir together yogurt and sugar until well blended.

NUTRIENTS PER SERVING			
Calories	120	Fat	3 g
Cholesterol	10 mg	Sodium	210 mg

Luscious Chocolate Cheesecake

Key Lime Cheesecake

CRUST

¾ cup crunchy nutlike cereal nuggets
¾ cup graham cracker crumbs
¼ cup Prune Purée (page 90) or prepared prune butter
3 tablespoons sugar

FILLING

1 package (8 ounces) fat free cream cheese, softened
1 can (14 ounces) low fat sweetened condensed milk
½ cup fresh lime juice
½ cup egg substitute
1 teaspoon grated lime peel
2 egg whites
⅛ teaspoon cream of tartar

TOPPING

⅔ cup low fat nondairy whipped topping
Lime slices and lime peel, for garnish

Preheat oven to 375°F. To prepare Crust, in food processor, process cereal, graham cracker crumbs, Prune Purée and sugar until well blended. Press onto bottom and part way up side of ungreased 8½- or 9-inch springform pan. To prepare Filling, in mixer bowl, beat cream cheese on medium speed until smooth. Gradually beat in condensed milk, lime juice, egg substitute and lime peel until blended. In small mixer bowl, with clean beaters, beat egg whites with cream of tartar until soft peaks form. Fold into cream cheese mixture. Pour into prepared crust. Bake in center of oven 20 to 25 minutes or until filling is set. Cool; refrigerate until cold. Cut into wedges. Top each serving with dollop of whipped topping. Garnish with lime slice and peel.

Makes 10 servings

Favorite recipe from **California Prune Board**

Key Lime Cheesecake

Cookies & Bars

• • • • • • • • • • •

Low Fat Molasses Jumbles

½ cup Prune Purée (page 90) or prepared prune butter
½ cup sugar
½ cup molasses
1 egg
2 cups all-purpose flour
2 teaspoons ground cinnamon
1 teaspoon ground ginger
½ teaspoon baking soda
½ teaspoon salt

Preheat oven to 350°F. Coat baking sheets with vegetable cooking spray. In large bowl, mix Prune Purée, sugar and molasses until well blended. Add egg; mix well. Combine remaining ingredients; stir into prune mixture just until blended. Roll heaping tablespoonfuls of dough in additional sugar. Place on baking sheets, spacing 2 inches apart. With fork, flatten dough in crisscross fashion until ½ inch thick. Bake in center of oven about 12 to 13 minutes or until set and bottoms are lightly browned. Remove from baking sheets to wire racks to cool completely.   *Makes 30 (2½-inch) cookies*

NUTRIENTS PER SERVING			
	(1 cookie)		
Calories	68	Fat	1 g
Cholesterol	7 mg	Sodium	57 mg

Favorite recipe from **California Prune Board**

Low Fat Molasses Jumbles

Chocolate Almond Biscotti

3 cups all-purpose flour
½ cup unsweetened cocoa
2 teaspoons DAVIS® Baking Powder
½ teaspoon salt
1 cup granulated sugar
⅔ cup FLEISCHMANN'S® Margarine, softened
¾ cup EGG BEATERS® Healthy Real Egg Product
1 teaspoon almond extract
½ cup whole blanced almonds, toasted and coarsely chopped
 Powdered Sugar Glaze (recipe follows)

In medium bowl, combine flour, cocoa, baking powder and salt. In large bowl, with electric mixer at medium speed, beat granulated sugar and margarine or until creamy. Add Egg Beaters® and almond extract; beat well. With mixer at low speed, gradually beat in flour mixture, just until blended; stir in almonds. On lightly greased baking sheet, form dough into two (12×2½-inch) logs. Bake at 350°F for 25 to 30 minutes or until toothpick inserted in centers comes out clean. Cool logs on wire racks 15 minutes.

Using serrated knife, slice each log diagonally into 12 (1-inch-thick) slices; place, cut sides up, on same baking sheet. Bake at 350°F for 12 to 15 minutes on each side or until crisp and browned. Cool completely on wire rack. Drizzle with Powdered Sugar Glaze. *Makes 2 dozen cookies*

Powdered Sugar Glaze: In small bowl, combine 1 cup powdered sugar and 5 to 6 teaspoons water until smooth.

Prep time: 25 minutes
Cook time: 45 minutes

NUTRIENTS PER SERVING			
(1 cookie)			
Calories	160	Fat	7 g
Cholesterol	0 mg	Sodium	125 mg

Chocolate Almond Biscotti

Gingersnaps

2½ cups all-purpose flour
1½ teaspoons ground ginger
1 teaspoon baking soda
1 teaspoon ground allspice
½ teaspoon salt
1½ cups sugar
2 tablespoons margarine, softened
½ cup MOTT'S® Apple Sauce
¼ cup GRANDMA'S® Molasses

1. Preheat oven to 375°F. Spray cookie sheets with nonstick cooking spray.

2. In medium bowl, sift together flour, ginger, baking soda, allspice and salt.

3. In large bowl, beat sugar and margarine with electric mixer at medium speed until blended. Whisk in apple sauce and molasses.

4. Add flour mixture to apple sauce mixture; stir until well blended.

5. Drop rounded tablespoonfuls of dough 1 inch apart onto prepared cookie sheets. Flatten each cookie slightly with moistened fingertips.

6. Bake 12 to 15 minutes or until firm. Cool completely on wire rack.

Makes 3 dozen cookies

NUTRIENTS PER SERVING			
(1 cookie)			
Calories	80	Fat	1 g
Cholesterol	0 mg	Sodium	60 mg

Top to bottom: Oatmeal Cookies (page 322),
Gingersnaps

Oatmeal Cookies

1   cup all-purpose flour
1   teaspoon baking powder
½   teaspoon baking soda
½   teaspoon salt
¼   cup MOTT'S® Cinnamon Apple Sauce
2   tablespoons margarine
½   cup granulated sugar
½   cup firmly packed light brown sugar
1   egg
1   teaspoon vanilla extract
1⅓   cups uncooked rolled oats
½   cup raisins (optional)

1. Preheat oven to 375°F. Spray cookie sheets with nonstick cooking spray.

2. In small bowl, combine flour, baking powder, baking soda and salt.

3. In large bowl, place apple sauce. Cut in margarine with pastry blender or fork until margarine breaks into pea-sized pieces. Add granulated sugar, brown sugar, egg and vanilla; stir until well blended.

4. Add flour mixture to apple sauce mixture; stir until well blended. Fold in oats and raisins, if desired.

5. Drop rounded teaspoonfuls of dough 2 inches apart onto prepared cookie sheets.

6. Bake 10 to 12 minutes or until lightly browned. Cool 5 minutes on cookie sheets. Remove to wire racks; cool completely.   *Makes 3 dozen cookies*

NUTRIENTS PER SERVING			
(1 cookie)			
Calories	60	Fat	1 g
Cholesterol	5 mg	Sodium	60 mg

322

Mocha Cookies

 2 tablespoons plus 1½ teaspoons instant coffee granules
1½ tablespoons skim milk
 ⅓ cup packed light brown sugar
 ¼ cup granulated sugar
 ¼ cup margarine
 1 egg
 ½ teaspoon almond extract
 2 cups all purpose flour, sifted
 ¼ cup wheat flakes
 ½ teaspoon ground cinnamon
 ¼ teaspoon baking powder

Preheat oven to 350°F. Spray cookie sheets with nonstick cooking spray.
Dissolve coffee granules in milk. In large bowl, beat brown sugar, granulated
sugar and margarine until smooth and creamy. Beat in egg, almond extract and
coffee mixture. Combine flour, wheat flakes, cinnamon and baking powder;
gradually beat flour mixture into sugar mixture. Drop by teaspoonfuls onto
prepared cookie sheets; flatten with back of fork. Bake 8 to 10 minutes.

Makes about 40 cookies

NUTRIENTS PER SERVING			
(1 cookie)			
Calories	48	Fat	1 g
Cholesterol	5 mg	Sodium	20 mg

Favorite recipe from **The Sugar Association, Inc.**

Cherry Chocolate Chip Walnut Cookies

1 cup sugar
¼ cup Prune Purée (page 90) or prepared prune butter *or* 1 jar
   (2½ ounces) first-stage baby food prunes
¼ cup water
2 tablespoons nonfat milk
1 teaspoon vanilla
½ teaspoon instant espresso coffee powder *or* 1 teaspoon
   instant coffee granules
1 cup all-purpose flour
½ cup unsweetened cocoa powder
¾ teaspoon baking soda
½ teaspoon salt
½ cup dried sour cherries
¼ cup chopped walnuts
¼ cup semisweet chocolate chips

Preheat oven to 350°F. Coat baking sheets with vegetable cooking spray. In large bowl, whisk together sugar, Prune Purée, water, milk, vanilla and espresso powder until mixture is well blended, about 1 minute. Combine flour, cocoa, baking soda and salt; mix into prune mixture until well blended. Stir in cherries, walnuts and chocolate chips. Spoon twelve equal mounds of dough onto prepared baking sheets, spacing at least 2 inches apart. Bake in center of oven 18 to 20 minutes or until set and tops of cookies feel dry to the touch. Cool on baking sheets 2 minutes; remove to wire rack to cool completely.

Makes 12 large cookies

NUTRIENTS PER SERVING			
(1 cookie)			
Calories	215	Fat	4 g
Cholesterol	0 mg	Sodium	180 mg

Favorite recipe from **California Prune Board**

Cherry Chocolate Chip Walnut Cookies

Soft Apple Cider Cookies

1 cup firmly packed light brown sugar
½ cup FLEISCHMANN'S® Margarine, softened
½ cup apple cider
½ cup EGG BEATERS® Healthy Real Egg Product
2¼ cups all-purpose flour
1½ teaspoons ground cinnamon
1 teaspoon baking soda
¼ teaspoon salt
2 medium apples, peeled and diced (about 1½ cups)
¾ cup PLANTER'S® Almonds, chopped
Cider Glaze (recipe follows)

In large bowl, with electric mixer at medium speed, beat sugar and margarine until creamy. Add cider and Egg Beaters®; beat until smooth. With electric mixer at low speed, gradually blend in flour, cinnamon, baking soda and salt. Stir in apples and almonds.

Drop dough by tablespoonfuls, 2 inches apart, onto greased baking sheets. Bake at 375°F for 10 to 12 minutes or until golden brown. Remove from sheets; cool on wire racks. Drizzle with Cider Glaze. *Makes 4 dozen cookies*

Cider Glaze: In small bowl, combine 1 cup powdered sugar and 2 tablespoons apple cider until smooth.

Prep time: 30 minutes
Cook time: 12 minutes

NUTRIENTS PER SERVING			
(1 cookie)			
Calories	80	Fat	3 g
Cholesterol	0 mg	Sodium	80 mg

Soft Apple Cider Cookies

Choco-Lowfat Strawberry Shortbread Bars

¼ cup (½ stick) (56 to 60% corn oil) spread
½ cup sugar
1 egg white
1¼ cups all-purpose flour
¼ cup HERSHEY®S Cocoa or HERSHEY®S European Style Cocoa
¾ teaspoon cream of tartar
½ teaspoon baking soda
   Dash salt
½ cup strawberry all-fruit spread
   Vanilla Chip Drizzle (recipe follows)

Heat oven to 375°F. Lightly spray 13×9×2-inch baking pan with vegetable cooking spray. Combine corn oil spread and sugar; beat on medium speed of electric mixer until well blended. Add egg white; beat until well blended. Mix flour, cocoa, cream of tartar, baking soda and salt; gradually add to sugar mixture. Gently press onto bottom of prepared pan. Bake 10 to 12 minutes or just until set. Cool in pan on wire rack. Spread fruit spread evenly over crust. Cut into bars or other shapes with cookie cutters. Prepare Vanilla Chip Drizzle; drizzle over tops of bars. Let stand until set. *Makes 36 bars*

VANILLA CHIP DRIZZLE

⅓ cup HERSHEY®S Vanilla Milk Chips
½ teaspoon shortening (do not use butter, margarine or oil)

In small microwave-safe bowl, place vanilla milk chips and shortening. Microwave at HIGH (100% power) 30 seconds; stir. If necessary, microwave at HIGH an additional 15 seconds at a time, stirring after each heating, just until chips are melted when stirred. Use immediately.

NUTRIENTS PER SERVING			
(1 bar with drizzle)			
Calories	50	Fat	1 g
Cholesterol	0 mg	Sodium	45 mg

Choco-Lowfat Strawberry Shortbread Bars

Tri-Layer Chocolate Oatmeal Bars

CRUST

1	cup uncooked rolled oats
½	cup all-purpose flour
½	cup firmly packed light brown sugar
¼	cup MOTT'S® Natural Apple Sauce
1	tablespoon margarine, melted
¼	teaspoon baking soda

FILLING

⅔	cup all-purpose flour
½	teaspoon baking powder
¼	teaspoon salt
¾	cup granulated sugar
¼	cup MOTT'S® Natural Apple Sauce
1	whole egg
1	egg white
2	tablespoons unsweetened cocoa powder
1	tablespoon margarine, melted
½	teaspoon vanilla extract
¼	cup low fat buttermilk

ICING

1	cup powdered sugar
1	tablespoon unsweetened cocoa powder
1	tablespoon skim milk
1	teaspoon instant coffee powder

1. Preheat oven to 350°F. Spray 8-inch square baking pan with nonstick cooking spray.

continued on page 332

Tri-Layer Chocolate Oatmeal Bars

330

Tri-Layer Chocolate Oatmeal Bars, continued

2. To prepare Crust, in medium bowl, combine oats, ½ cup flour, brown sugar, ¼ cup apple sauce, 1 tablespoon margarine and baking soda. Stir with fork until mixture resembles coarse crumbs. Press evenly into bottom of prepared pan. Bake 10 minutes.

3. To prepare Filling, in small bowl, combine ⅔ cup flour, baking powder and salt.

4. In large bowl, combine granulated sugar, ¼ cup apple sauce, whole egg, egg white, 2 tablespoons cocoa, 1 tablespoon margarine and vanilla.

5. Add flour mixture to apple sauce mixture alternately with buttermilk; stir until well blended. Spread filling over baked crust.

6. Bake 25 minutes or until toothpick inserted in center comes out clean. Cool completely on wire rack.

7. To prepare Icing, in small bowl, combine powdered sugar, 1 tablespoon cocoa, milk and coffee powder until smooth. Spread evenly over bars. Let stand until set. Run tip of knife through icing to score. Cut into 14 bars.

Makes 14 servings

NUTRIENTS PER SERVING			
Calories	190	Fat	3 g
Cholesterol	15 mg	Sodium	100 mg

PHILLY® FREE® Marble Brownies

  1 package (20½ ounces) reduced calorie brownie mix
  1 package (8 ounces) PHILADELPHIA BRAND® FREE® Fat
       Free Cream Cheese, softened
 ⅓ cup sugar
  1 egg
 ½ teaspoon vanilla
  1 cup BAKER'S® Semi-Sweet Real Chocolate Chips

PREPARE brownie mix as directed on package. Pour into 13×9-inch baking pan that has been sprayed with nonstick cooking spray.

BEAT cream cheese with electric mixer on medium speed until smooth. Add sugar, mixing until blended. Add egg and vanilla; mix just until blended.

POUR cream cheese mixture over brownie mixture; cut through batter with knife several times for marble effect. Sprinkle with chips.

BAKE at 350°F for 35 to 40 minutes or until cream cheese mixture is lightly browned. Cool; cut into squares. *Makes 24 servings*

Prep time: 20 minutes
Baking time: 40 minutes

Cappuccino Brownies: Dissolve 1 tablespoon MAXWELL HOUSE® Instant Coffee in 1 tablespoon water. Stir coffee mixture into cream cheese mixture. Continue as directed.

NUTRIENTS PER SERVING			
Calories	130	Fat	3 g
Cholesterol	20 mg	Sodium	80 mg

Fruit and Nut Bars

1   cup unsifted all-purpose flour
1   cup quick oats
⅔   cup brown sugar
2   teaspoons baking soda
½   teaspoon salt
½   teaspoon cinnamon
⅔   cup buttermilk
3   tablespoons vegetable oil
2   large egg whites, lightly beaten
1   Golden Delicious apple, cored and chopped
½   cup dried cranberries or raisins, chopped
¼   cup chopped nuts
2   tablespoons flaked coconut (optional)

1. Heat oven to 375°F. Lightly grease 9-inch square baking pan. In large mixing bowl, combine flour, oats, brown sugar, baking soda, salt and cinnamon; stir to blend.

2. Add buttermilk, oil and egg whites; beat with electric mixer just until mixed. Stir in apple, dried fruit and nuts; spread evenly in pan and top with coconut, if desired. Bake 20 to 25 minutes or until cake tester inserted in center comes out clean. Cool and cut into 10 bars.   *Makes 10 bars*

NUTRIENTS PER SERVING			
Calories	232	Fat	7 g
Cholesterol	1 mg	Sodium	298 mg

Favorite recipe from Washington Apple Commission

Fruit and Nut Bars

Bamboozlers

1 cup all-purpose flour
¾ cup packed light brown sugar
¼ cup unsweetened cocoa powder
1 egg
2 egg whites
5 tablespoons margarine, melted
¼ cup skim milk
¼ cup honey
1 teaspoon vanilla
2 tablespoons semisweet chocolate chips
2 tablespoons coarsely chopped walnuts
   Powdered sugar (optional)

1. Preheat oven to 350°F. Grease and flour 8-inch square baking pan; set aside. Combine flour, brown sugar and cocoa in medium bowl. Blend together egg, egg whites, margarine, milk, honey and vanilla in medium bowl. Add to flour mixture; mix well. Pour into prepared baking pan; sprinkle with chocolate chips and walnuts.

2. Bake brownies until they spring back when lightly touched in center, about 30 minutes. Cool completely in pan on wire rack. Sprinkle with powdered sugar just before serving. *Makes 12 servings*

Peanutters: Substitute peanut butter chips for chocolate chips and peanuts for walnuts.

Brownie Sundaes: Top each brownie with a scoop of vanilla nonfat frozen yogurt and 2 tablespoons nonfat chocolate or caramel sauce.

NUTRIENTS PER SERVING			
Calories	188	Fat	7 g
Cholesterol	18 mg	Sodium	79 mg

Pumpkin Harvest Bars

1¾ cups all-purpose flour
2 teaspoons baking powder
1 teaspoon grated orange peel
1 teaspoon ground cinnamon
½ teaspoon salt
½ teaspoon ground nutmeg
¼ teaspoon ground ginger
¼ teaspoon ground cloves
¾ cup sugar
½ cup MOTT'S® Natural Apple Sauce
½ cup solid-pack pumpkin
1 whole egg
1 egg white
2 tablespoons vegetable oil
½ cup raisins

1. Preheat oven to 350°F. Spray 13×9-inch baking pan with nonstick cooking spray.

2. In small bowl, combine flour, baking powder, orange peel, cinnamon, salt, nutmeg, ginger and cloves.

3. In large bowl, combine sugar, apple sauce, pumpkin, whole egg, egg white and oil.

4. Add flour mixture to apple sauce mixture; stir until well blended. Stir in raisins. Spread batter into prepared pan.

5. Bake 25 to 30 minutes or until toothpick inserted in center comes out clean. Cool on wire rack 15 minutes; cut into 16 bars. *Makes 16 servings*

NUTRIENTS PER SERVING			
Calories	130	Fat	2 g
Cholesterol	15 mg	Sodium	110 mg

Pumpkin Harvest Bars

Fruit and Oat Squares

1 cup all-purpose flour
1 cup uncooked quick oats
¾ cup packed light brown sugar
½ teaspoon baking soda
¼ teaspoon salt
¼ teaspoon ground cinnamon
⅓ cup margarine or butter, melted
¾ cup apricot, cherry or other fruit flavor preserves

1. Preheat oven to 350°F. Spray 9-inch square baking pan with nonstick cooking spray; set aside.

2. Combine flour, oats, brown sugar, baking soda, salt and cinnamon in medium bowl; mix well. Add margarine; stir with fork until mixture is crumbly.

3. Reserve ¾ cup crumb mixture for topping. Press remaining crumb mixture evenly onto bottom of prepared pan. Bake 5 to 7 minutes or until lightly browned.

4. Spread preserves onto crust; sprinkle with reserved crumb mixture.

5. Bake 20 to 25 minutes or until golden brown. Cool completely in pan on wire rack. Cut into 16 squares. *Makes 16 servings*

NUTRIENTS PER SERVING			
Calories	161	Fat	4 g
Cholesterol	0 mg	Sodium	123 mg

340

Desserts

● ● ● ● ● ● ● ● ● ● ●

Apple Strudel

1　sheet (½ of a 17¼-ounce package) frozen puff pastry
1　cup (4 ounces) shredded ALPINE LACE® Reduced Fat
　　Cheddar Cheese
2　large Granny Smith apples, peeled, cored and sliced ⅛ inch
　　thick (12 ounces)
⅓　cup golden raisins
2　tablespoons apple brandy (optional)
¼　cup granulated sugar
¼　cup packed light brown sugar
½　teaspoon ground cinnamon
2　tablespoons unsalted butter substitute, melted

1. To shape the pastry: Thaw the pastry for 20 minutes. Preheat the oven to 350°F. On a floured board, roll the pastry into a 15×12-inch rectangle.

2. To make the filling: Sprinkle the cheese on the dough, leaving a 1-inch border. Arrange the apples on top. Sprinkle with the raisins, then the brandy, if you wish. In a small cup, mix both of the sugars with the cinnamon, then sprinkle over the apple filling.

3. Starting from one of the wide ends, roll up jelly-roll style. Place on a baking sheet, seam side down, tucking the ends under. Using a sharp knife, make 7 diagonal slits on the top, then brush with the butter. Bake for 35 minutes or until golden brown.

Makes 18 servings

NUTRIENTS PER SERVING			
Calories	151	Fat	8 g
Cholesterol	6 mg	Sodium	123 mg

Easy Fruit Tarts

12 wonton skins
    Vegetable cooking spray
 2 tablespoons apple jelly or apricot fruit spread
1½ cups sliced or cut-up fruit such as DOLE® Bananas,
    Strawberries, Raspberries or Red or Green Seedless Grapes
 1 cup nonfat or low fat yogurt, any flavor

• **Press** wonton skins into 12 muffin cups sprayed with vegetable cooking spray, allowing corners to stand over edges of muffin cups.

• **Bake** at 375°F 5 minutes or until lightly browned. Carefully remove wonton cups to wire rack; cool.

• **Cook** and stir jelly in small saucepan over low heat until jelly melts.

• **Brush** bottoms of cooled wonton cups with melted jelly. Place two fruit slices in each cup; spoon rounded tablespoon of yogurt on top of fruit. Garnish with fruit slice and mint leaves. Serve immediately.   *Makes 12 servings*

Prep time: 20 minutes
Bake time: 5 minutes

NUTRIENTS PER SERVING			
Calories	55	Fat	0 g
Cholesterol	1 mg	Sodium	60 mg

Easy Fruit Tarts

Chocolate-Filled Meringue Shells with Strawberry Sauce

2 egg whites
¼ teaspoon cream of tartar
Dash salt
¾ cup sugar
¼ teaspoon vanilla extract
Chocolate Filling (recipe follows)
1 package (10 ounces) frozen strawberries in syrup, thawed

Heat oven to 275°F. Line 10 muffin cups (2½ inches in diameter) with paper bake cups. In small bowl, beat egg whites with cream of tartar and salt until soft peaks form. Beat in sugar, 1 tablespoon at a time, beating well after each addition until stiff peaks hold their shape and mixture is glossy. Fold in vanilla. Spoon about 3 tablespoons mixture in each muffin cup. Using back of spoon, push mixture up sides of muffin cups to form well in center.

Bake 1 hour or until meringues turn delicate cream color and feel dry to the touch. Cool in pan on wire rack. Before serving, carefully remove paper from shells. For each serving, spoon 1 heaping tablespoonful Chocolate Filling into meringue shell. In blender container, place strawberries with syrup. Blend until smooth. Spoon over filled shells. Store leftover shells loosely covered at room temperature. *Makes 10 servings*

Chocolate Filling: In small bowl, beat 4 ounces softened Neufchâtel cheese (light cream cheese) and ¼ cup HERSHEY®S Cocoa on medium speed of electric mixer until blended. Gradually add ¾ cup powdered sugar. Fold in 1 cup frozen light non-dairy whipped topping, thawed.

NUTRIENTS PER SERVING			
Calories	170	Fat	4 g
Cholesterol	10 mg	Sodium	95 mg

Chocolate-Filled Meringue Shells
with Strawberry Sauce

346

Pumpkin Apple Tart

CRUST

1	cup plain dry bread crumbs
1	cup crunchy nut-like cereal nuggets
½	cup sugar
½	teaspoon ground cinnamon
½	teaspoon ground nutmeg
¼	cup MOTT'S® Natural Apple Sauce
2	tablespoons margarine, melted
1	egg white

FILLING

12	ounces evaporated skim milk
1½	cups solid-pack pumpkin
⅔	cup sugar
½	cup MOTT'S® Chunky Apple Sauce
⅓	cup GRANDMA'S® Molasses
2	egg whites
1	whole egg
½	teaspoon ground ginger
½	teaspoon ground cinnamon
½	teaspoon ground nutmeg
	Frozen light nondairy whipped topping, thawed (optional)

1. Preheat oven to 375°F. Spray 9- or 10-inch springform pan with nonstick cooking spray.

2. **To prepare Crust,** in medium bowl, combine bread crumbs, cereal, ½ cup sugar, ½ teaspoon cinnamon and ½ teaspoon nutmeg.

3. Add ¼ cup apple sauce, margarine and egg white; mix until moistened. Press onto bottom of prepared pan.

continued on page 350

Pumpkin Apple Tart

Pumpkin Apple Tart, continued

4. Bake 8 minutes.

5. **To prepare Filling,** place evaporated milk in small saucepan. Cook over medium heat until milk almost boils, stirring occasionally.

6. In large bowl, combine evaporated milk, pumpkin, ⅔ cup sugar, ½ cup chunky apple sauce, molasses, 2 egg whites, whole egg, ginger, ½ teaspoon cinnamon and ½ teaspoon nutmeg. Pour into baked crust.

7. *Increase oven temperature to 400°F.* Bake 35 to 40 minutes or until center is set.

8. Cool 20 minutes on wire rack. Remove side of pan. Spoon or pipe whipped topping onto tart, if desired. Cut into 12 slices. Refrigerate leftovers.

Makes 12 servings

NUTRIENTS PER SERVING			
Calories	210	Fat	3 g
Cholesterol	20 mg	Sodium	170 mg

SMUCKER'S® Double Apple Turnovers

½ cup SMUCKER'S® Apple Butter
½ cup apple cider or juice
½ teaspoon ground cinnamon
　 Grated peel of 1 orange
¼ cup golden raisins
4 large firm apples, peeled, cored and chopped
1 package frozen phyllo dough
　 Nonstick cooking spray
　 Granulated sugar for garnish

Preheat oven to 375°F. Place Smucker's® Apple Butter, cider, cinnamon and orange peel in a pot and simmer for 5 minutes. Add the raisins and heat for 2 minutes more. Add the apples; cook over medium heat for about 10 minutes or until the apples begin to soften and most of the liquid evaporates. Cool in refrigerator.

Unwrap the phyllo dough. Remove one sheet of dough, keeping remaining sheets covered with damp cloth. Coat dough with cooking spray, then cover with a second sheet of dough. Spray top sheet with cooking spray.

Spoon about ⅓ cup of the apple filling on the lower right corner of the dough. Fold the dough over the filling to form a large rectangle. Then fold the turnover as if it were a flag, making a triangular packet with each turn. Repeat process with remaining dough and filling until 6 turnovers are made. Place finished turnovers on a baking sheet. Sprinkle turnovers with granulated sugar before baking. Bake approximately 25 minutes until golden. *Makes 6 turnovers*

Prep time: 30 minutes
Cook time: 40 minutes

NUTRIENTS PER SERVING			
Calories	214	Fat	1 g
Cholesterol	0 mg	Sodium	2 mg

351

Tiramisu

3 cups water
3 tablespoons honey
1 cup instant nonfat dry milk
2 tablespoons cornstarch
⅛ teaspoon ground cloves
¼ teaspoon ground cinnamon
⅛ teaspoon salt
½ cup cholesterol-free egg substitute
½ cup espresso coffee
2 tablespoons orange extract
12 ladyfingers, cut in half lengthwise
¼ cup grated semisweet chocolate

1. Bring water and honey to a boil in medium saucepan over high heat. Reduce heat; simmer, uncovered, 20 minutes. Remove from heat.

2. Combine dry milk, cornstarch, cloves, cinnamon and salt in medium bowl. Slowly add milk mixture to honey mixture, stirring until smooth. Bring to a boil, stirring constantly, over medium heat. Remove from heat.

3. Pour egg substitute into small bowl. Add ½ cup hot milk mixture to egg substitute; blend well. Stir egg mixture back into remaining milk mixture in saucepan. Cook over low heat 2 minutes or until thickened. Cool 15 minutes. Combine coffee with orange extract in another small bowl. Set aside.

4. Arrange 6 ladyfingers in 1-quart serving bowl. Drizzle half the coffee mixture over ladyfingers. Spread half the custard over ladyfingers. Sprinkle with half the grated chocolate. Repeat layers; cover and refrigerate 2 hours. Spoon into individual bowls. Garnish if desired. *Makes 6 servings*

NUTRIENTS PER SERVING			
Calories	223	Fat	5 g
Cholesterol	82 mg	Sodium	167 mg

Fresh Fruit with Peach Glaze

2   cups DOLE® Orchard Peach, Pine-Orange-Guava, Pineapple
     Orange, Pine-Orange-Banana, Mandarin Tangerine or
     Country Raspberry Juice
3   tablespoons sugar
1   tablespoon cornstarch
1   tablespoon lemon juice
½   teaspoon grated lemon peel
8   cups cut-up fresh fruit, such as DOLE® Fresh Pineapple,
     Bananas, Strawberries, Red or Green Seedless Grapes,
     Cantaloupe, Oranges, Peaches, Nectarines or Kiwi

• **Combine** peach juice, sugar, cornstarch, lemon juice and lemon peel in medium saucepan.

• **Cook** and stir over medium-high heat 5 minutes or until mixture comes to boil. Reduce heat to low; cook 2 minutes or until slightly thickened. Cool slightly. Sauce can be served warm or chilled.

• **Arrange** fruit in dessert dishes. Spoon glaze over fruit. Refrigerate any leftovers in air-tight container. Garnish with fresh mint leaves, if desired.

Makes 8 servings

Prep time: 5 minutes
Cook time: 5 minutes

NUTRIENTS PER SERVING			
Calories	125	Fat	0 g
Cholesterol	0 mg	Sodium	19 mg

Fresh Fruit with Peach Glaze

Baked Apple Crisp

    8   cups unpeeled, thinly sliced apples (about 8 medium)
    2   tablespoons granulated sugar
 1½   tablespoons lemon juice
    4   teaspoons ground cinnamon, divided
 1½   cups MOTT'S® Natural Apple Sauce
    1   cup uncooked rolled oats
  ½   cup firmly packed light brown sugar
  ⅓   cup all-purpose flour
  ⅓   cup evaporated skim milk
  ¼   cup nonfat dry milk powder
    1   cup vanilla nonfat yogurt

1. Preheat oven to 350°F. Spray 2-quart casserole dish with nonstick cooking spray.

2. In large bowl, toss apple slices with granulated sugar, lemon juice and 2 teaspoons cinnamon. Spoon into prepared dish. Spread apple sauce evenly over apple mixture.

3. In medium bowl, combine oats, brown sugar, flour, evaporated milk, dry milk powder and remaining 2 teaspoons cinnamon. Spread over apple sauce.

4. Bake 35 to 40 minutes or until lightly browned and bubbly. Cool slightly; serve warm. Top each serving with dollop of yogurt.   *Makes 12 servings*

NUTRIENTS PER SERVING			
Calories	185	Fat	2 g
Cholesterol	0 mg	Sodium	35 mg

Baked Apple Crisp

Sweet Holidays Pizza

Sweet Crumb Crust (recipe follows)
1½ pints (3 cups) vanilla or other desired flavor nonfat frozen
yogurt, slightly softened
1½ pints (3 cups) chocolate or other desired flavor nonfat frozen
yogurt, slightly softened
1 cup canned or fresh pineapple chunks
6 whole fresh strawberries, cut in half
1 cup thawed frozen peach slices *or* 1 medium peach, peeled
and sliced
1 kiwi, peeled and sliced
12 pecan halves (optional)
¼ cup nonfat chocolate syrup, heated nonfat chocolate fudge
sauce or favorite fruit flavored ice cream topping

1. Prepare Sweet Crumb Crust; freeze 15 minutes.

2. Spread yogurts onto crust to within ½ inch of edge. Cover with plastic wrap; freeze until firm, 6 hours or overnight.

3. Arrange fruits and nuts decoratively on top of pizza just before serving. Drizzle with chocolate syrup. Cut into wedges to serve.   *Makes 16 servings*

SWEET CRUMB CRUST

2 cups graham cracker or vanilla wafer cookie crumbs
¼ cup sugar
¾ teaspoon ground cinnamon
6 tablespoons margarine, melted

1. Line 12-inch pizza pan with aluminum foil; set aside.

2. Combine crumbs, sugar and cinnamon in medium bowl; stir in margarine. Place in prepared pizza pan; press mixture evenly onto bottom of pan.

continued on page 360

Sweet Holidays Pizza, continued

Rocky Road Pizza: Omit vanilla frozen yogurt and fruits. Increase chocolate frozen yogurt to 1½ quarts (6 cups). Substitute 3 tablespoons chopped dry roasted peanuts for pecan halves. Prepare crust as directed. Spread yogurt onto crust as directed; cover and freeze until firm. Sprinkle with ¾ cup miniature marshmallows. Drizzle with nonfat chocolate syrup.

Spumoni Pizza: Omit fruits. Reduce chocolate and vanilla frozen yogurts to 2 cups *each.* Add 2 cups slightly softened strawberry frozen nonfat yogurt. Substitute 3 tablespoons toasted slivered almonds for pecan halves. Prepare crust as directed. Spread yogurts onto crust; freeze until firm. Top with ½ cup *each* halved red and green maraschino cherries; sprinkle with almonds. Drizzle with nonfat chocolate syrup or strawberry ice cream topping.

Sweet Valentine Pizza: Omit chocolate syrup. Prepare crust as directed. Substitute 1½ quarts (6 cups) strawberry nonfat frozen yogurt for the chocolate and vanilla frozen yogurts, and ½ to ¾ cup halved fresh strawberries for assorted fresh fruits. Drizzle with nonfat chocolate syrup or strawberry ice cream topping.

NUTRIENTS PER SERVING			
Calories	302	Fat	8 g
Cholesterol	0 mg	Sodium	230 mg

Light Banana Cream Pie

1 package (1.9 ounces) sugar-free vanilla instant pudding and
 pie filling (four ½-cup servings)
2¾ cups low fat milk
4 ripe, medium DOLE® Bananas, sliced
1 (9-inch) ready-made graham cracker pie crust
1 firm, medium DOLE® Banana (optional)
 Light frozen non-dairy whipped topping, thawed (optional)

• **Prepare** pudding as directed using 2¾ cups low fat milk. Stir in 4 sliced ripe bananas.

• **Spoon** banana mixture into pie crust. Place plastic wrap over pie, lightly pressing plastic to completely cover filling. Chill 1 hour or until filling is set. Remove plastic wrap.

• **Cut** firm banana into ½-inch slices. Garnish pie with whipped topping and banana slices.   *Makes 8 servings*

Prep time: 10 minutes
Chill time: 1 hour

NUTRIENTS PER SERVING			
Calories	199	Fat	6 g
Cholesterol	3 mg	Sodium	242 mg

361

Rice Pudding

1¼ cups water, divided
½ cup uncooked long-grain rice
2 cups evaporated skim milk
½ cup granulated sugar
½ cup raisins
½ cup MOTT'S® Natural Apple Sauce
3 tablespoons cornstarch
1 teaspoon vanilla extract
Brown sugar or nutmeg (optional)
Fresh raspberries (optional)
Orange peel strips (optional)

1. In medium saucepan, bring 1 cup water to a boil. Add rice. Reduce heat to low and simmer, covered, 20 minutes or until rice is tender and water is absorbed.

2. Add milk, granulated sugar, raisins and apple sauce. Bring to a boil. Reduce heat to low and simmer for 3 minutes, stirring occasionally.

3. Combine cornstarch and remaining ¼ cup water in small bowl. Stir into rice mixture. Simmer about 20 minutes or until mixture thickens, stirring occasionally. Remove from heat; stir in vanilla. Cool 15 to 20 minutes before serving. Sprinkle each serving with brown sugar or nutmeg and garnish with raspberries and orange peel, if desired. Refrigerate leftovers.

Makes 8 servings

NUTRIENTS PER SERVING			
Calories	190	Fat	1 g
Cholesterol	2 mg	Sodium	75 mg

Rice Pudding

Microwave Chocolate Pudding

⅓ cup sugar
¼ cup unsweetened cocoa powder
2 tablespoons cornstarch
1½ cups 2% low-fat milk
1 teaspoon vanilla
⅛ teaspoon ground cinnamon (optional)
   Assorted small candies (optional)

1. Combine sugar, cocoa powder and cornstarch in medium microwavable bowl or 1-quart glass measure. Gradually add milk, stirring with wire whisk until well blended.

2. Microwave at HIGH 2 minutes; stir. Microwave at MEDIUM-HIGH (70%) 3½ to 4½ minutes or until thickened, stirring every 1½ minutes.

3. Stir in vanilla and cinnamon. Let stand at least 5 minutes before serving, stirring occasionally to prevent skin from forming. Serve warm or chilled. Garnish with candies just before serving, if desired.   *Makes 4 servings*

NUTRIENTS PER SERVING			
Calories	139	Fat	2 g
Cholesterol	7 mg	Sodium	50 mg

Blueberry Bread Pudding with Caramel Sauce

8 slices white bread, cubed
1 cup fresh or frozen blueberries
2 cups skim milk
1 cup EGG BEATERS® Healthy Real Egg Product
⅔ cup sugar
1 teaspoon vanilla extract
¼ teaspoon ground cinnamon
Caramel Sauce (recipe follows)

Place bread cubes in bottom of lightly greased 8×8×2-inch baking pan. Sprinkle with blueberries; set aside.

In large bowl, combine milk, Egg Beaters®, sugar, vanilla and cinnamon; pour over bread mixture. Set pan in larger pan filled with 1-inch depth hot water. Bake at 350°F for 1 hour or until knife inserted in center comes out clean. Serve warm with Caramel Sauce. *Makes 9 servings*

Caramel Sauce: In small saucepan, over low heat, heat ¼ cup skim milk and 14 vanilla caramels until caramels are melted, stirring frequently.

Prep time: 20 minutes
Cook time: 1 hour

NUTRIENTS PER SERVING			
Calories	210	Fat	2 g
Sodium	227 mg	Cholesterol	2 mg

Blueberry Bread Pudding with Caramel Sauce

Frozen Chocolate-Covered Bananas

2 ripe medium bananas
4 wooden sticks
½ cup low-fat granola cereal without raisins
⅓ cup hot fudge sauce, at room temperature

1. Cover baking sheet or 15×10-inch jelly-roll pan with waxed paper; set aside.

2. Peel bananas; cut each in half crosswise. Insert wooden stick into center of cut end of each banana, about 1½ inches into banana half. Place on prepared baking sheet; freeze until firm, at least 2 hours.

3. Place granola in large resealable plastic food storage bag; crush slightly using rolling pin or meat mallet. Transfer granola to shallow plate. Place fudge sauce in shallow dish.

4. Working with 1 banana at a time, place frozen banana in fudge sauce; turn banana and spread fudge sauce evenly onto banana with small rubber scraper. Immediately place banana on plate with granola; turn to coat lightly. Return to baking sheet in freezer. Repeat with remaining bananas.

5. Freeze until fudge sauce is very firm, at least 2 hours. Place on small plates; let stand 5 minutes before serving. *Makes 4 servings*

NUTRIENTS PER SERVING			
Calories	163	Fat	4 g
Cholesterol	0 mg	Sodium	25 mg

Fudge Brownie Sundaes

 1 cup all-purpose flour
 ¾ cup granulated sugar
 ½ cup unsweetened cocoa powder, divided
 2 teaspoons baking powder
 ½ teaspoon salt
 ½ cup skim milk
 ¼ cup MOTT'S® Natural Apple Sauce
 1 teaspoon vanilla extract
 1¾ cups hot water
 ¾ cup firmly packed light brown sugar
 ½ gallon frozen nonfat vanilla yogurt
    Maraschino cherries (optional)

1. Preheat oven to 350°F. Spray 8-inch square baking pan with nonstick cooking spray.

2. In large bowl, combine flour, granulated sugar, ¼ cup cocoa, baking powder and salt. Add milk, apple sauce and vanilla; stir until well blended. Pour batter into prepared pan.

3. In medium bowl, combine hot water, brown sugar and remaining ¼ cup cocoa. Pour over batter. *Do not stir.*

4. Bake 40 minutes or until center is almost set. Cool completely on wire rack. Cut into 12 bars. Top each bar with ½-cup scoop of frozen yogurt; spoon sauce from bottom of pan over yogurt. Garnish with cherry, if desired.

Makes 12 servings

NUTRIENTS PER SERVING			
Calories	300	Fat	3 g
Cholesterol	5 mg	Sodium	200 mg

Fudge Brownie Sundae

Chocolate-Banana Sherbet

2 ripe medium bananas
1 cup apricot nectar or peach or pineapple juice, divided
½ cup HERSHEY'S Semi-Sweet Chocolate Chips
2 tablespoons sugar
1 cup lowfat 2% milk

Into blender container or food processor, slice bananas. Add ¾ cup apricot nectar. Cover; blend until smooth. In small microwave-safe bowl, place chocolate chips, remaining ¼ cup apricot nectar and sugar. Microwave at HIGH (100%) 30 seconds; stir. If necessary, microwave at HIGH an additional 15 seconds at a time, stirring after each heating, just until chips are melted and mixture is smooth when stirred. Add to banana mixture in blender. Cover; blend until thoroughly combined. Add milk. Cover; blend until smooth. Pour into 8- or 9-inch square pan. Cover; freeze until hard around edges, about 2 hours.

Into large mixer bowl or food processor, spoon partially frozen mixture; beat until smooth but not melted. Return mixture to pan. Cover; freeze until firm, stirring several times before mixture freezes. Before serving, let stand at room temperature 10 to 15 minutes until slightly softened. Scoop into 8 individual dessert dishes.

Makes 8 servings

NUTRIENTS PER SERVING			
Calories	130	Fat	4 g
Cholesterol	5 mg	Sodium	15 mg

Acknowledgments

• • • • • • • • •

The publisher would like to thank the companies and organizations listed below for the use of their recipes and photographs in this publication.

Alpine Lace Brands, Inc.
American Lamb Council
California Prune Board
California Tree Fruit Agreement
Delmarva Poultry Industry, Inc.
Dole Food Company, Inc.
Florida Department of Citrus
Golden Grain/Mission Pasta
Grandma's Molasses, a division of Cadbury Beverages Inc.
Guiltless Gourmet, Inc.
Healthy Choice®
Heinz U.S.A.
Hershey Foods Corporation
Kraft Foods, Inc.
Louis Rich Company
McIlhenny Company
Minnesota Cultivated Wild Rice Council
MOTT'S® U.S.A., a division of Cadbury Beverages Inc.
Nabisco, Inc.
National Broiler Council
National Cattlemen's Beef Association
National Fisheries Institute
National Pork Producers Council
National Turkey Federation
Nestlé Food Company
Norseland, Inc.
Perdue Farms Incorporated
The Procter & Gamble Company
Sargento Foods Inc.®
The J.M. Smucker Company
StarKist Seafood Company
The Sugar Association, Inc.
USA Rice Council
Washington Apple Commission

Index

METRIC CONVERSION CHART

VOLUME MEASUREMENTS (dry)

⅛ teaspoon = 0.5 mL
¼ teaspoon = 1 mL
½ teaspoon = 2 mL
¾ teaspoon = 4 mL
1 teaspoon = 5 mL
1 tablespoon = 15 mL
2 tablespoons = 30 mL
¼ cup = 60 mL
⅓ cup = 75 mL
½ cup = 125 mL
⅔ cup = 150 mL
¾ cup = 175 mL
1 cup = 250 mL
2 cups = 1 pint = 500 mL
3 cups = 750 mL
4 cups = 1 quart = 1 L

VOLUME MEASUREMENTS (fluid)

1 fluid ounce (2 tablespoons) = 30 mL
4 fluid ounces (½ cup) = 125 mL
8 fluid ounces (1 cup) = 250 mL
12 fluid ounces (1½ cups) = 375 mL
16 fluid ounces (2 cups) = 500 mL

WEIGHTS (mass)

½ ounce = 15 g
1 ounce = 30 g
3 ounces = 90 g
4 ounces = 120 g
8 ounces = 225 g
10 ounces = 285 g
12 ounces = 360 g
16 ounces = 1 pound = 450 g

DIMENSIONS

1/16 inch = 2 mm
⅛ inch = 3 mm
¼ inch = 6 mm
½ inch = 1.5 cm
¾ inch = 2 cm
1 inch = 2.5 cm

OVEN TEMPERATURES

250°F = 120°C
275°F = 140°C
300°F = 150°C
325°F = 160°C
350°F = 180°C
375°F = 190°C
400°F = 200°C
425°F = 220°C
450°F = 230°C

BAKING PAN SIZES

Utensil	Size in Inches/Quarts	Metric Volume	Size in Centimeters
Baking or	8×8×2	2 L	20×20×5
Cake Pan	9×9×2	2.5 L	22×22×5
(square or	12×8×2	3 L	30×20×5
rectangular)	13×9×2	3.5 L	33×23×5
Loaf Pan	8×4×3	1.5 L	20×10×7
	9×5×3	2 L	23×13×7
Round Layer	8×1½	1.2 L	20×4
Cake Pan	9×1½	1.5 L	23×4
Pie Plate	8×1¼	750 mL	20×3
	9×1¼	1 L	23×3
Baking Dish	1 quart	1 L	—
or Casserole	1½ quart	1.5 L	—
	2 quart	2 L	—